# Chief Executive
# SUCCESSION
# PLANNING

## Essential Guidance for Boards and CEOs

### SECOND EDITION

## Nancy R. Axelrod

BOARDSOURCE®
*Building Effective Nonprofit Boards*

Library of Congress Cataloging-in-Publication Data

Axelrod, Nancy R.

  Chief executive succession planning : essential guidance for boards and CEOs / Nancy R. Axelrod. -- 2nd ed.

      p. cm.

  ISBN 1-58686-114-X

1.  Chief executive officers--Selection and appointment. 2.  Nonprofit organizations--Management.  I. BoardSource (Organization) II. Title.

  HF5549.5.R44A92 2009

  658.4'0701--dc22                           2009044717

© 2010 BoardSource.
First Printing, November 2009
ISBN 1-58686-114-X

Published by BoardSource
1828 L Street, NW, Suite 900
Washington, DC 20036

The views in each BoardSource publication are those of its author, and do not represent official positions of BoardSource or its sponsoring organizations. Information and guidance in this book is provided with the understanding that BoardSource is not engaged in rendering professional opinions. If such opinions are required, the services of an attorney should be sought.

**BOARDSOURCE**®
*Building Effective Nonprofit Boards*

BoardSource is dedicated to advancing the public good by building exceptional nonprofit boards and inspiring board service.

BoardSource was established in 1988 by the Association of Governing Boards of Universities and Colleges (AGB) and Independent Sector (IS). Prior to this, in the early 1980s, the two organizations had conducted a survey and found that although 30 percent of respondents believed they were doing a good job of board education and training, the rest of the respondents reported little, if any, activity in strengthening governance. As a result, AGB and IS proposed the creation of a new organization whose mission would be to increase the effectiveness of nonprofit boards.

With a lead grant from the Kellogg Foundation and funding from five other donors, BoardSource opened its doors in 1988 as the National Center for Nonprofit Boards with a staff of three and an operating budget of $385,000. On January 1, 2002, BoardSource took on its new name and identity. These changes were the culmination of an extensive process of understanding how we were perceived, what our audiences wanted, and how we could best meet the needs of nonprofit organizations.

Today, BoardSource is the premier voice of nonprofit governance. Its highly acclaimed products, programs, and services mobilize boards so that organizations fulfill their missions, achieve their goals, increase their impact, and extend their influence. BoardSource is a 501(c)(3) organization.

## BoardSource provides

- resources to nonprofit leaders through workshops, training, and an extensive Web site (www.boardsource.org)

- governance consultants who work directly with nonprofit leaders to design specialized solutions to meet an organization's needs

- the world's largest, most comprehensive selection of material on nonprofit governance, including a large selection of books and CD-ROMs

- an annual conference that brings together approximately 900 governance experts, board members, and chief executives and senior staff from around the world

For more information, please visit our Web site at www.boardsource.org, e-mail us at mail@boardsource.org, or call us at 800-883-6262.

# Have You Used These BoardSource Resources?

## THE GOVERNANCE SERIES

1. *Ten Basic Responsibilities of Nonprofit Boards, Second Edition*
2. *Legal Responsibilities of Nonprofit Boards, Second Edition*
3. *Financial Responsibilities of Nonprofit Boards, Second Edition*
4. *Fundraising Responsibilities of Nonprofit Boards, Second Edition*
5. *The Nonprofit Board's Role in Mission, Planning, and Evaluation, Second Edition*
6. *Structures and Practices of Nonprofit Boards, Second Edition*

## BOOKS

*Chief Executive Transitions: How to Hire and Support a Nonprofit CEO*

*Assessment of the Chief Executive*

*Nonprofit Executive Compensation: Planning, Performance, and Pay, Second Edition*

*Trouble at the Top: The Nonprofit Board's Guide to Managing an Imperfect Chief Executive*

*The Board Chair Handbook, Second Edition*

*Navigating the Organizational Lifecycle: A Capacity-Building Guide for Nonprofit Leaders*

*Getting the Best from Your Board: An Executive's Guide to a Successful Partnership*

*Taming the Troublesome Board Member*

*Moving Beyond Founder's Syndrome to Nonprofit Success*

*Culture of Inquiry: Healthy Debate in the Boardroom*

*Governance as Leadership: Reframing the Work of Nonprofit Boards*

*Understanding Nonprofit Financial Statements, Third Edition*

*The Nonprofit Board Answer Book: A Practical Guide for Board Members and Chief Executives, Second Edition*

*The Board Building Cycle: Nine Steps to Finding, Recruiting, and Engaging Nonprofit Board Members, Second Edition*

*The Nonprofit Dashboard: A Tool for Tracking Progress*

*Financial Committees*

*The Nonprofit Legal Landscape*

*The Nonprofit Board's Guide to Bylaws*

*Managing Conflicts of Interest: A Primer for Nonprofit Boards, Second Edition*

*The Nonprofit Policy Sampler, Second Edition*

*The Source: Twelve Principles of Governance That Power Exceptional Boards*

*Fearless Fundraising for Nonprofit Boards, Second Edition*

*Driving Strategic Planning: A Nonprofit Executive's Guide, Second Edition*

*Who's Minding the Money? An Investment Guide for Nonprofit Board Members, Secoond Edition*

## DVDs

*Meeting the Challenge: An Orientation to Nonprofit Board Service*

*Speaking of Money: A Guide to Fundraising for Nonprofit Board Members*

## ONLINE ASSESSMENTS

*Board Self-Assessment*

*Assessment of the Chief Executive*

*Executive Search — Needs Assessment*

For an up-to-date list of publications and information about current prices, membership, and other services, please call BoardSource at 800-883-6262 or visit our Web site at www.boardsource.org. For consulting services, please e-mail us at consulting@boardsource.org or call 877-892-6293.

# CONTENTS

**CHAPTER 1: SUCCESSION PLANNING PRECEDES EXECUTIVE TRANSITIONS . . . . . . . 1**
The Difference Between Executive Transition and Succession Planning . . . . . 2
Succession Planning Should Be Proactive . . . . . . . . . . . . . . . . . . . . . . . . . . . . 2
The Chief Executive Succession Planning Cycle . . . . . . . . . . . . . . . . . . . . . . 5

**CHAPTER 2: FIVE KEY SUCCESSION PLANNING STEPS
PRIOR TO THE EXECUTIVE SEARCH . . . . . . . . . . . . . . . . . . . . . . . . . . . . . . . . . 7**
Step 1. Understand the Job of the Nonprofit Chief Executive . . . . . . . . . . . . 7
Step 2. Develop an Emergency Leadership Transition Management Plan . . . . . 8
Step 3. Define the Mutual Expectations of the Chief Executive
and the Board . . . . . . . . . . . . . . . . . . . . . . . . . . . . . . . . . . . . . . . . . . . . . . . . 10
Step 4. Design and Implement a Constructive and Humane Process
for Evaluating the Chief Executive's Performance . . . . . . . . . . . . . . . . . . . . 13
Step 5. Develop a Productive Process for Board Self-Assessment . . . . . . . . . 17
Create the Conditions for the Chief Executive to Succeed . . . . . . . . . . . . . . 18

**CHAPTER 3: DETERMINING WHERE THE ORGANIZATION WANTS TO GO
PRIOR TO AN EXECUTIVE TRANSITION . . . . . . . . . . . . . . . . . . . . . . . . . . . . . . 21**
Survey the Stakeholders . . . . . . . . . . . . . . . . . . . . . . . . . . . . . . . . . . . . . . . . 22
Organizational Assessment Questions That Determine the Context for
Upcoming Chief Executive Leadership Transitions . . . . . . . . . . . . . . . . . . . . 23

**CHAPTER 4: SIX KEY ISSUES FOR THE BOARD TO ADDRESS
DURING THE EXECUTIVE SEARCH . . . . . . . . . . . . . . . . . . . . . . . . . . . . . . . . . 31**
1. Define the Core Leadership and Management Competencies . . . . . . . . . . 31
2. Create the Chief Executive Profile . . . . . . . . . . . . . . . . . . . . . . . . . . . . . . 39
3. Consider Hiring an Interim Chief Executive . . . . . . . . . . . . . . . . . . . . . . 40
4. Develop a Communications Plan . . . . . . . . . . . . . . . . . . . . . . . . . . . . . . . 42
5. Define the Role of the Outgoing Chief Executive
   in Succession Planning . . . . . . . . . . . . . . . . . . . . . . . . . . . . . . . . . . . . . . 43
6. Avoid Five Common Pitfalls During the Executive Search . . . . . . . . . . . . 45

**CHAPTER 5: HIRING THE CHIEF EXECUTIVE DOES NOT COMPLETE
THE SUCCESSION PLANNING PROCESS . . . . . . . . . . . . . . . . . . . . . . . . . . . . . 49**
Consider a Leadership Transition Team . . . . . . . . . . . . . . . . . . . . . . . . . . . . 49
Provide a Formal Orientation Program for the Chief Executive . . . . . . . . . . . 50
Encourage the New Chief Executive to Conduct Informational Interviews . . 52
Agree on Written Goals and Expectations for the Chief Executive . . . . . . . . . 53
Consider an Executive Coach for the New Chief Executive . . . . . . . . . . . . . 54
Warning Signals of Inadequate Succession Planning . . . . . . . . . . . . . . . . . . . 56

**APPENDIX 1: EMERGENCY LEADERSHIP TRANSITION PLAN** . . . . . . . . . . . . . . . . . . **59**

**APPENDIX 2: CHIEF EXECUTIVE SUCCESSION PLAN GUIDELINES** . . . . . . . . . . . . . **61**

**APPENDIX 3: A SAMPLE CHIEF EXECUTIVE PROFILE** . . . . . . . . . . . . . . . . . . . . . . **63**

**SUGGESTED RESOURCES** . . . . . . . . . . . . . . . . . . . . . . . . . . . . . . . . . . . . . . . **67**

**ABOUT THE AUTHOR** . . . . . . . . . . . . . . . . . . . . . . . . . . . . . . . . . . . . . . . . . . **69**

# CHAPTER 1

## *SUCCESSION PLANNING PRECEDES EXECUTIVE TRANSITIONS*

Chief executive leadership transitions are pivotal points that exert a profound impact on organizational performance. This is why the selection, evaluation, and retention of the right leader are widely proclaimed as the board's most important role. But boards typically neglect this three-part role until a chief executive must be replaced. The announcement from the incumbent executive that he or she wishes to move on, a sudden or unexpected departure, or the awareness of the need for new leadership are occasions that prompt boards to leap into the choreography of an executive search.

But this leap comes too late. Failure to plan for succession well in advance of the executive search can result in chaos when a chief executive abruptly departs or passes away. It can create costly delays in organizational momentum and progress and needlessly raise a sense of uncertainty on the part of many board and staff members. Effective nonprofit boards understand that while chief executive departures are often unexpected, executive leadership turnover is inevitable. The best way to ensure a smooth and successful executive transition is to anticipate it and to plan for it. The manner in which a board navigates any executive leadership transition will be influenced by how effective it has been in creating the conditions for a successful executive leadership transition well before the search process has been activated.

An example of a succession planning strategy is to develop a list of competencies needed in the chief executive before the next executive transition. The board of a large international professional society established a task force to do this. The task force was charged with engaging board and staff members, key volunteers, and other leaders to identify the essential leadership competencies that would be most critical to advancing the organization's mission and vision over the next five years. It was clear to the board and the chief executive that these competencies would inform the board self-assessment process, the chief executive performance review, and a potential search committee if an executive transition were to occur during the next few years.

## THE DIFFERENCE BETWEEN EXECUTIVE TRANSITION AND SUCCESSION PLANNING

If the board wants to lay the groundwork for a successful transition to new leadership, it should invest in the forethought and advance work known as succession planning. While internal candidates are often considered during nonprofit executive searches, "succession planning" in this text does not refer to the more common practice in the private sector of grooming an "heir apparent" from the management team to become the next chief executive. While boards and chief executives should ensure that continuous leadership development opportunities are available within the organization to grow emerging leaders, the board must ultimately decide which candidate — from within or outside the organization — will provide the best fit for the organization at the time of the executive search.

The difference between chief executive selection and chief executive succession underscores the importance of why it is important for boards to start now. The search for a new chief executive is an intermittent event that is timeline-driven. Succession planning, on the other hand, reflects an ongoing, continuous process that boards (with the help of their chief executive) implement to

1. create the conditions for the incumbent chief executive to succeed

2. understand the organization's current and future strategy

3. ensure that a sound infrastructure is in place whenever the search for the next chief executive is launched

The search for and selection of the chief executive is typically the most labor-intensive part of an executive transition. But it is only one component of the succession plan. While this book provides guidance on selective parts of the executive search and selection phase, readers at organizations required to hire a chief executive will find *Chief Executive Transitions: How to Hire and Support a Nonprofit CEO* by Don Tebbe (BoardSource, 2008) helpful for this critical part of the succession planning process.

## SUCCESSION PLANNING SHOULD BE PROACTIVE

This book has been written to help a board take a proactive rather than a reactive approach to chief executive leadership transitions. As illustrated in the "Chief Executive Succession Planning Cycle," some of the steps described in this guide, such as clarifying expectations of the chief executive and the board and assessing the performance of the chief executive, should be revisited as needed as ongoing succession planning mechanisms. Other components of succession planning, such as the type of institutional assessment offered in this guide and other steps within the executive search phase, will be activated by specific events, such as the incumbent chief executive's expected or unexpected departure.

*Chief Executive Succession Planning: Essential Guidance for Boards and CEOs* is written primarily for two types of nonprofit leaders: board members and (outgoing and incoming) chief executives. The former are ultimately responsible for selecting, supporting, and evaluating the chief executive. The latter should be concerned with matters of legacy and succession. Succession planning works best when board members and the incumbent chief executive collaborate in advance in a purposeful manner to create the conditions for a successful executive leadership transition — whether or not it is expected in the near future. In practice, this is not possible if either party defaults on its obligation to put the organization's interests above its own.

The event of an executive search should be included in a succession plan. Before a board can attract and retain the right chief executive, the board must determine the needs of the organization. This continuum for chief executive succession planning begins with a fundamental understanding of the job of the nonprofit chief executive, the need for an emergency executive transition plan, the benefits of an assessment process for the chief executive and the board, and the board's intention to actively create a climate in which the chief executive can succeed.

## SUCCESSION PLANNING TRIGGERS

Events that should prompt the board (ideally with the new chief executive) to either create a new succession plan or revisit the process to ensure that it is current and on track include

- the transition to a new board chair

- the performance evaluation for the chief executive

- the board self-assessment process

- the beginning of a new strategic planning cycle

- any breakdown or crisis involving the chief executive

- significant turnover in board composition

- significant turnover in staff

- a founder chief executive or board member who has "outstayed" his or her effectiveness

Many things contribute to the effectiveness of the succession planning process for chief executives. The following chapters of this book address four important dimensions of chief executive succession planning.

Chapter Two describes significant succession planning steps the board can take well before a leadership transition is contemplated to support effective executives.

Before a board can embark on an executive transition, it must have a clear understanding of the values, needs, and priorities of the organization. The institutional assessment diagnostic tool in Chapter Three can be used to help the board identify the leadership and management competencies that will inform the development of a chief executive profile and executive search plan.

Chapter Four outlines key succession planning issues the board should be mindful of during the executive search phase, such as linking the competencies sought in the next chief executive to the needs of the organization and designing a communications strategy to keep the community informed.

Chapter Five describes key succession planning strategies once the executive search phase of the chief executive succession cycle has been completed with the appointment of the new chief executive.

## CHIEF EXECUTIVE SUCCESSION PLANNING CYCLE

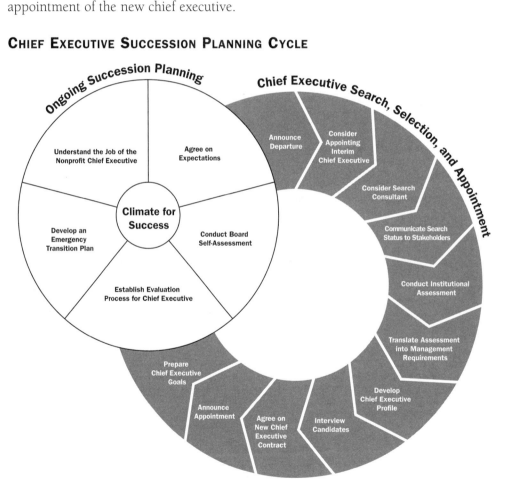

# THE CHIEF EXECUTIVE SUCCESSION PLANNING CYCLE

Boards will navigate chief executive leadership transitions more successfully by anticipating a continuum of succession planning steps that starts rather than ends with the selection of the chief executive. This is why the first succession planning steps addressed in this book revolve around enhancing communications and strengthening the relationship between the board and the current chief executive.

Because succession planning is a continuous process that is not sparked by a specific event, it cannot be as easily reduced to a one-size-fits-all model plan. As a result, the steps described in this guide are not necessarily linear. The important thing is to attend to the specific steps (such as a regular review of the chief executive's performance) and to make the process ongoing, aligned with the organization's needs, and adaptive to changing conditions. Readers are encouraged to create their own customized timelines to link succession planning steps with the needs, circumstances, and leadership variables at their organizations. For example, organizations with founding chief executives may find it especially critical or challenging to have frequent, candid discussions about planning for the founder's successor.

Readers are encouraged to review the whole guide before determining the right sequence of steps and the timeline that will be most responsive to the unique circumstances and variables within their organization. Boards that are ready to conduct an executive search will find practical advice and sample practices to carry out this critical stage of succession planning in *Chief Executive Transitions: How to Hire and Support a Nonprofit CEO* by Don Tebbe (BoardSource, 2008).

## SUCCESSION PLANNING POINTS TO REMEMBER

- Prepare for chief executive transitions before they occur.
- Understand the difference between chief executive search and succession planning.
- Approach succession planning as an ongoing and adaptive process rather than a specific event.
- Start the succession planning process as soon as the new chief executive is appointed.
- If a succession plan has not been developed, use succession planning triggers to start the process.

# CHAPTER 2

## FIVE KEY SUCCESSION PLANNING STEPS PRIOR TO THE EXECUTIVE SEARCH

The need has never been greater for boards to provide the framework of support and accountability that allows a chief executive to succeed. Just as chief executives will influence the nature and level of engagement of their boards in meeting their responsibilities, boards play a prime role in the performance, satisfaction, and term of the chief executive. There are a number of things that board members should understand, respect, and act on to implement an effective succession plan before an executive search looms on the horizon.

### STEP 1. UNDERSTAND THE JOB OF THE NONPROFIT CHIEF EXECUTIVE

Serving as the chief executive of a nonprofit organization can be both satisfying and grueling. Like most institutional chief professional officers, chief executives must play multiple roles, cope with complexity and uncertainty, embody their organization's mission, and guide the vision. Like most leaders, they are expected to do a lot in a little time, make tough and often unpopular decisions, understand the needs and concerns of a wide range of institutional stakeholders, and model the behavior and values expected of others.

Unlike their counterparts in the private sector, they manage organizations that are accountable to the public trust, and earnings-per-share does not constitute a key performance metric. Nonprofit chief executives tend to allocate greater portions of their time searching for capital to finance their organization's work and pleading for investments in infrastructure that are readily accepted (if not financed) as requirements for the production and delivery of products and services in the for-profit world.

The multiple dimensions of the demands placed on the modern nonprofit chief executive should encourage boards to take a closer look at what keeps many of them awake at night or quietly determined to limit their time of service. These pressures can exact an intellectual and emotional toll on a chief executive and his or her family. Too many executives do not use all their vacation time due to their workload. Boards that find ways to help their executives manage the stresses that come with the position, compensate them fairly, and provide a climate for them to succeed are likely to secure a greater return on their investment in succession planning.

According to the results of surveys of nonprofit executives conducted by CompassPoint Nonprofit Services and the Bridgespan Group, a number of senior-level executives will leave their jobs over the next few years. Many of these departures will be a result of baby boomer executives who plan to retire or move into other careers. And yet, chief executives and board members do not share quite the same perceptions regarding executive turnover. While 49 percent of chief executives anticipate a change in their position within the next five years, only 30 percent of board members see this change coming (BoardSource's *Nonprofit Governance Index 2007*).

The CompassPoint study revealed that most chief executives planning to leave their current positions do not want another senior-level job. This is ascribed to these positions' long hours and high stress levels, especially over organization finances. While boards are unlikely to face a shortage of aspirants for chief executive positions, according to the Bridgespan report, the greatest obstacles to filling senior-level positions are insufficient compensation, a lack of candidates with specialized skills, and inadequate career paths for managers within nonprofit organizations.

Hospitals, higher education institutions, and larger nonprofits generally pay higher chief executive salaries than smaller organizations. While salaries (as well as tenures) vary widely depending on the size, type, and revenue sources of nonprofit organizations, a recent Urban Institute survey confirms that "nonprofit chief executives earn relatively small salaries compared with other occupations" — "despite the consistent challenges of running organizations."

## STEP 2. DEVELOP AN EMERGENCY LEADERSHIP TRANSITION MANAGEMENT PLAN

One of the most unsettling events in the life of an organization is a change within the top professional position. Even when it is planned, the stakes and the uncertainty are high. When it is not planned, there is a greater chance the actions taken to deal with the sudden, unexpected absence of the chief executive will be hasty, ill considered, and needlessly alarming to the organization's stakeholders. In case an event renders the chief executive unable to perform essential duties, the board should have an emergency transition management contingency plan in place to foster continuity and ensure stability during this time.

Organizations that gracefully weather an abrupt chief executive departure are more likely to have boards that have anticipated what needs to be done to ensure the well-being of the organization and its stakeholders. An effective emergency leadership management plan provides clarity on who will do what in the event that the chief executive cannot perform his or her essential duties. Having the following information in one place will provide board members with the tools and the contacts they need to ensure effective management during an unexpected leadership transition.

### A. Communications Plan

Who is the first point of contact in the event of a change in the chief executive's situation? (Typically, this would be the board chair.)

This person should be prepared to notify all board members and discuss next steps.

Subsequent communication containing the circumstances and recommended plan of action should be sent to all board members for approval and to the staff for information.

Once the plan of action has been determined, a message from the board chair should be sent to the organization's key stakeholders detailing the plan.

### B. Financial Oversight

Having multiple signatories on the organization's checking accounts enables business to continue in the chief executive's absence. These signatories might include the board chair and the secretary-treasurer (who could also be included on the investment account).

To account for geographical differences, it should be possible to make transactions electronically on all of the accounts.

Contact information for financial advisors should be available for questions related to financial issues.

Contact information for accountants (internal and external) should be available to ensure that timely employee payroll payments are continued.

Other critical information and contact lists that should be available to the board chair in the event of an emergency (e.g., contact information for key funders and upcoming deadlines on key activities, such as the deadline for filing the IRS Form 990.)

### C. Interim Management

Who will the board designate to perform the chief executive's essential duties while it conducts a search for a new chief executive? Should this be determined in advance for short-term periods (e.g., three months) versus longer term periods? Two options for interim management are

1. An acting chief executive appointed by the board to provide leadership during the planning and or implementation phases of the executive search. This might be a senior manager or a board member.

2. An interim chief executive who helps prepare the organization to work effectively with the next chief executive. This might be a seasoned executive from outside of the organization.

### D. Executive Search

While interim management is in place, is the board likely to work with an executive search consultant? If so, what are the best sources of recommendations on qualified search consultants for the board to consider?

What action will the board take to appoint a search committee?

What is the proper delegation of authority between the search committee and the board?

Portions of an emergency leadership transition management plan can be tested when the chief executive takes a vacation, a sabbatical, or some other time away from the organization. This can provide a good opportunity to observe the mettle of emerging leaders within the organization.

## STEP 3. DEFINE THE MUTUAL EXPECTATIONS OF THE CHIEF EXECUTIVE AND THE BOARD

### A CONSTRUCTIVE PARTNERSHIP

"Exceptional boards recognize that they cannot govern well without the chief executive's collaboration and that the chief executive cannot lead the organization to its full potential without the board's unflagging support."

*The Source: Twelve Principles of Governance That Power Exceptional Boards,* BoardSource, 2005.

Succession planning is never static. The players keep changing as board members, board officers, and chief executives come and go. As organizations undergo changes in institutional strategy, environmental conditions, and people, boards and chief executives need to communicate regularly about the expectations they have of one another. This dialogue should not be deferred until performance evaluation time rolls around for the chief executive, but it often is. Chief executive performance reviews, as well as board self-assessments, are important steps in the succession planning cycle. They allot a time and a forum for the board and the chief executive to reflect on how well each party is meeting its responsibilities.

A board contributes to a successful and effective chief executive in several ways: by clarifying expectations, by linking the executive to key leaders, by charging the executive to build an effective leadership team and facilitate visionary thinking, and by not undermining a chief executive through the personal agendas of individual board members. Forging a healthy relationship between the chief executive and board chair in which each is willing to challenge and support the other takes time and trust.

It is especially important to revisit expectations when the chief executive or the board finds that there is too much ambiguity surrounding their roles or when a conscious effort is needed to clarify respective roles in areas in which more than one group has authority. Clarity on mutual expectations between the board and the chief executive does not necessarily eliminate gray areas. But both parties should be conscious of the scope and nature of their authority, especially in overlapping areas. Board members who chronically micromanage or bring personal agendas can seriously undermine a chief executive's authority and credibility.

While the players, the environment, and the rules of engagement are likely to change, the need for a strong, constructive relationship between the board and the chief executive does not. The chief executive depends on the board for the authority to function and to manage the organization. The best executives work to enlist the collective wisdom board members bring to decisions about institutional mission, direction, and values. One of the most critical variables in succession planning is the way in which the chief executive and board work together — how they share governance responsibilities, how readily they exchange relevant information, the degree to which they can simultaneously support and challenge each other, and the chemistry between them.

CompassPoint recently found that chief executives who have been on the job for 15 or more years have spent, at several points in their tenures, up to 25 percent of their time building and managing their boards. In high-performing organizations, the board and the chief executive are a team responsible for one another's well-being and success and adroitly make use of the tension between mutual support and accountability. "But when the board side of the team is weaker than the executive side, too many executives respond by making their boards less relevant and important. Successful executives know that building a governing and supporting board takes their genuine commitment, time, and leadership, and they willingly accept that responsibility."

*Daring to Lead 2006: A National Study of Nonprofit Executive Leadership*

The dirty secret in executive transitions is that a striking number of chief executives depart as a result of unarticulated feuds with board members. These disagreements can simmer beneath the surface for long periods of time until they are defined with shattering clarity when the chief executive resigns or is dismissed. Dueling chief executives and boards should not be consigned to live together indefinitely. They should find civil ways to bring their disputes to the surface in order to diagnose the underlying conflicts — before the conflicts undermine governance. In some cases, little things may be symptomatic of something more serious. In other cases, seemingly major disputes turn out to be proxies for superficial differences that can be easily resolved.

Tensions that arise as board members try to understand what actions constitute responsible oversight versus unproductive interference — or appropriate delegation of responsibility to the chief executive versus snoring on the job — can't be resolved with simple ditties such as "The board makes policy and the staff executes it." Dynamic tension between the board and the chief executive is natural. It can be healthy when it is tempered by robust communication and a willingness to share different views and address conflicts.

An overbearing founder can also be a succession planning trigger point. At an organization that experienced high growth and heavy dependence on private funding, the chief executive was highly regarded for her role in the organization's success. Unfortunately, in addition to approaching burnout from 24/7 fundraising and other responsibilities, she was frustrated by the unreasonable expectations of a founder who demanded more from her and her staff than the organization could sustain given its priorities. Because the board was unwilling to call the founder on inappropriate requests and to reassure the chief executive that she was on track, she decided to leave her job out of sheer physical and mental exhaustion. When she informed the board of her decision to depart, she couched it in terms of wanting to pursue another career. The board was devastated. There is a good chance that the board could have retained this executive if a) she had felt safe talking about her problems with either the board chair or another board member she trusted, b) board officers had taken the initiative to inquire periodically about her health and morale, or c) board leaders had not abdicated their responsibility to provide guidance to the overbearing founder and support to the chief executive in taking the organizational reins away from the founder.

## WHAT CAN BOARD MEMBERS DO FOR SUCCESSION PLANNING FOR FOUNDING CHIEF EXECUTIVES?

An organization's greatest asset is often also its greatest liability. The highly successful founder turns into a potential liability the moment she leaves. Whether the departure is planned or unplanned doesn't matter.

1. Practice "succession thinking." This term signifies the kind of work that should occur before more formal succession planning. Boards that engage in succession thinking are always contemplating the stage of the organization's leadership — even if the founder's departure isn't imminent. Is there an obvious successor among the executives and managers who report directly to the chief executive? More immediately, is there anyone in the group who is qualified to step into the interim chief executive position if there was a sudden vacancy? If the answer is no, the organization faces a distinct risk. It takes a deliberate effort for the chief executive to prepare someone to take over from her, and there are no shortcuts. Begin planning for a vacancy now, and a sudden opening will never take the board by surprise.

2. Confirm the organizational strategy. If there is not a workable, clearly understood strategy in place for the organization, take steps to develop one now. It is virtually impossible to succeed at replacing a founder — at least the first time — without a strategic plan.

3. Discuss needs and expectations. What characteristics should the new chief executive have? What skills and personality traits fit best with the future direction?

4. Review the retirement plan. If there is none, try to start one. Having retirement benefits is the best a nonprofit can do in lieu of generous severance agreements. Consult a qualified benefits planning consultant to begin this process. Be aware that retirement plan or not, deferred compensation options can be used to build a least a modest retirement nest egg for a departing founder if the planning starts early enough.

*Moving Beyond Founder's Syndrome to Nonprofit Success* by Thomas McLaughlin and Addie Nelson Backlund, BoardSource, 2008.

The following sections on performance evaluation for the chief executive and self-assessment for the board describe two important succession planning mechanisms that help clarify roles and revisit mutual expectations between the chief executive and the board.

## STEP 4. DESIGN AND IMPLEMENT A CONSTRUCTIVE AND HUMANE PROCESS FOR EVALUATING THE CHIEF EXECUTIVE'S PERFORMANCE

Agreeing in advance on a formal chief executive assessment process as part of the succession planning process provides a framework for a regular dialogue between the board and the chief executive. Ideally, this agreement on the process to be used is reached at the time the chief executive is selected. By doing so, no one is surprised later.

In the best of all worlds, boards and chief executives should not have to wait until performance evaluation time to discuss mutual expectations and institutional priorities. In fact, a board strengthens the succession planning process by offering constructive feedback at regular intervals rather than waiting until an annual review. The more that board members and chief executives talk along the way, the easier it to address conflicts and affirm accomplishment when the official review time comes along. In practice, there have been many occasions when known leadership problems were not addressed until a crisis erupted — a sure recipe for launching a popularity contest rather than a thoughtful process of reviewing the chief executive's strengths and areas for improvement.

The need for the board to formally and periodically assess the chief executive's performance is neglected almost as often as it is touted. There are reasons for this. First in the absence of an up-to-date job description, a list of annual institutional goals, and the chief executive's individual performance goals (established in advance by the board and the chief executive), the board lacks uniform, baseline criteria to review the executive's performance. Second, many board members (as well as chief executives) are reluctant to move out of their comfort zones to exchange candid feedback — or even to evaluate a successful chief executive because of the discomfort that typically surrounds any performance feedback.

"Boards should not underestimate their role in chief executive job satisfaction. Many chief executives find boards personally helpful and a resource rather than an obstacle for getting things done. Chief executives who have a written evaluation are more satisfied with their jobs. Furthermore, chief executives who give their boards an effective rating have greater job satisfaction than those who give their boards an ineffective rating."

*BoardSource Governance Index 2007.*

While a performance assessment is an opportunity to discuss problems, the overarching purposes of the process should be to clarify goals for the chief executive and the organization, to foster the growth of the chief executive, and to provide constructive feedback. A scheduled systematic chief executive evaluation process can also assign a more objective time to address relevant succession planning issues. For example, it presents an opportunity for the board to assess how well the chief executive is building leadership within the organization. Some boards ask their chief executives to develop leadership development plans and to allocate the resources to groom future administrators who have the potential to become chief executive candidates for their current organization or others.

### "WHAT IF NANCY WERE RUN OVER BY A TRUCK TOMORROW?"

During my tenure as a nonprofit chief executive, my board chair once confided to me that in the periodic executive sessions I encouraged my board to have without my presence, an individual would often ask, "What if Nancy were run over by a truck tomorrow?" I told the board chair that I welcomed an opportunity to discuss with the board some of the things I was doing to create a strong infrastructure that worked regardless of who served as the chief executive. The responses to this blunt but relevant question can help a board and chief executive periodically review and update its emergency leadership transition management plan as well as its succession plan.

The assessment process can also provide a diplomatic opening for the board and chief executive to discuss the future leadership needs of the organization. Is there a need for new leadership? Does the chief executive desire to make a career change, retire, or serve the organization in another capacity? What is the timing for an executive transition that will best serve the organization's needs?

An example of a graceful ending occurred at a large professional society where the chief executive had shared with the board his desire to retire within the next two years. The board and the chief executive were reluctant to volunteer this information to the staff or members for a number of reasons. The organization had just gone through a major governance restructure, the association's membership profile was changing, and there were major public policy issues on the horizon that demanded the chief executive's credibility and outreach skills for resolution. Therefore, the chief executive and board met with a facilitator with leadership transition skills to discuss the implications of a leadership transition, the best timing for the search process, and the issues that needed to be addressed prior to the announcement of the search. They developed a comprehensive, timed communications plan to inform members, government leaders, partner organizations, and other stakeholders about the upcoming leadership transition and the steps in the process at the appropriate time.

A good succession planning process like this can help bring a successful chief executive's tenure to a graceful end. Even when there is mutual agreement between the board and the chief executive, the executive leadership transition must be carefully planned. But some chief executives may want to stay on beyond their effectiveness because they do not wish to leave. It is the board's responsibility to help the chief executive determine when he or she has achieved core goals and brought the organization to its next stage of development. If this discussion is embedded in a regular executive performance assessment process, this can reduce the chance of surprises. When the chief executive is not leaving voluntarily, certain occasions may require the board to carefully orchestrate a process that helps him or her leave with grace and dignity without compromising the organization's interests.

*Daring to Lead 2006: A National Study of Nonprofit Executive Leadership* revealed that a high percentage of executives depart via forced resignations. The report notes that "This rough ending to tenures that may well have been successful at earlier points might be avoided if executives were to periodically examine their current job fit. Executive directors should continually ask themselves: Am I the person to manage the challenges emerging for this organization and to take it to the next level of mission achievement? Would this organization and I be better off if I took my experience and abilities to a different service perch in the community? These questions should be part of the dialogue that occurs with the board as it conducts the executive director's annual performance assessment."

A formal, periodic performance evaluation process allows the chief executive to model the accountability he or she typically requires from the rest of the staff and to identify opportunities and challenges with the board. The best evaluation processes provide the board with a forum to express support and to make suggestions on areas for improvement. They should lower the probability of launching an evaluation only when the chief executive is in trouble. Once areas of improvement are identified, the intervention the board and chief executive agree upon may require greater self-awareness by the chief executive, greater support from the board, the addition of a staff or consultant such as an executive coach, or a professional development program.

The good news is that a growing number of boards conduct chief executive performance assessments. According to the BoardSource's *Nonprofit Governance Index 2007,* 74 percent of chief executives have a formal, written evaluation by the board. The bad news is that it is not always done well. Impediments to a constructive and humane chief executive performance assessment include

- implementing a performance review in response to a crisis

- making it a perfunctory, meaningless exercise

- not inviting the chief executive to

  o help shape the process

  o conduct a self-assessment

- delegating the board's responsibility to other constituents

- breaching confidentiality

- waiting until the assessment process to consider accomplishments or problems

- waiting too long to share the results of the performance assessment with the chief executive

- not inviting every member of the board to contribute feedback on the executive's performance

- not providing feedback to the board on the results of the performance assessment

## KEY OBJECTIVES OF CHIEF EXECUTIVE PERFORMANCE ASSESSMENT

In *Assessment of the Chief Executive* (BoardSource, 2005), authors Joshua Mintz and Jane Pierson highlight the following three goals of a chief executive assessment process:

1. Clarify expectations between the board and the chief executive on roles, responsibilities, and job expectation.

2. Provide insight into the board's perception of the executive's strengths, limitations, and overall performance.

3. Foster the growth and development of both the chief executive and the organization.

Mintz and Pierson provide a practical tool for a comprehensive assessment, which might be instituted every two to three years and can be customized. Included in the tool is an abridged questionnaire that might be more effective before a new chief executive completes his or her first year or other occasions when a less comprehensive assessment is necessary.

# STEP 5. DEVELOP A PRODUCTIVE PROCESS FOR BOARD SELF-ASSESSMENT

The prospect of selecting a new chief executive illuminates the quality of the board's effectiveness and its performance. Boards that suffer from passivity, complacency, insularity, or meddlesome behavior are less likely to encourage the best candidates during the executive search. They may also find it difficult to retain the best and brightest chief executives.

A good board periodically asks itself if it is doing the right work in the right way. A hallmark of effective succession planning is a regular, periodic process for reviewing and strengthening the board's effectiveness. Boards that have engaged in continuous learning and self-improvement are not only better positioned to attract qualified candidates during the executive search, they are more likely to anticipate and navigate a leadership transition.

## BOARD SELF-ASSESSMENT OPTIONS

One of the characteristics of effective boards that emerged in the early governance research conducted by Richard Chait, Barbara Taylor, and Tom Holland is that "they consciously create opportunities for board education and development and regularly seek information and feedback on the board's own performance. They pause periodically for self-reflection, to assess strengths and limitations, and to examine and learn from the board's mistakes. (*The Effective Board of Trustees,* Rowman and Littlefield Education, 1991)

Board self-assessment approaches range from the informal to the formal. Mechanisms for board evaluation include

- board meeting evaluations
- discussion of critical incidents that provide teachable moments for the board to learn from its breakdowns or breakthroughs
- exit interviews with board members at the end of their terms
- mini board self-assessment questionnaires
- formal board self-assessment tools (such as the BoardSource instruments)

Like a formal evaluation of the chief executive, one of the advantages of a regular board self-assessment process is that it schedules a time and a discipline to strengthen the board's performance. Individual board members can be remarkably forthright about the board's strengths and limitations if they are given a safe means of reflecting on whether they are doing the right work, how the board can add the greatest value, and what areas of board operation need improvement. Many boards have found it useful to take the time to engage in a formal board self-assessment process that gives board members an opportunity to be candid and introspective without fear of awkwardness or compromising themselves.

Boards use a variety of tools and processes for assessment. Some design their own. Others use questionnaires created by organizations such as BoardSource. Some ask consultants to design customized questionnaires. Some use questionnaires, interviews, or both. When the board decides to invest time in formal board self-assessment, the process produces better results when the full board commits to the process, when clear and relevant questions are framed, and when the information from the self-assessment is used for developmental purposes rather than as a report card. Outside facilitators can be used to relieve the board chair or chief executive of chairing the meeting to review the results and to help the board develop a plan of action to follow through on the results.

Too many board members are over surveyed and underengaged. Board self-assessment should not be undertaken if it is a perfunctory exercise. It should not be a mechanical process where board members are merely asked to check off compliance measures and nod to formulaic benchmarks. If the board is not willing to take action and make changes revealed in the self-assessment to improve the board's structure, culture, or practices, it is better not to do it at all.

The conventional wisdom is that the board should formally assess the chief executive's performance annually and conduct a formal review of its own performance every two to three years. In recognition of how difficult it is to evaluate the chief executive without a commensurate review of the board (and vice versa), some organizations integrate and link both processes. Whether chief executive and board assessments are done unilaterally or concurrently, the challenge is to design simple and relevant assessment tools that are expected to yield substantive results.

## CREATE THE CONDITIONS FOR THE CHIEF EXECUTIVE TO SUCCEED

More than any others, board members exert the greatest influence in creating the conditions to help chief executives do what they were ostensibly hired to do. Performance review of both the board and the chief executive provides critical succession planning opportunities to clarify goals for the organization, the chief executive, and the board. Whether the board uses performance assessments to support and nurture the chief executive, to provide opportunities for constructive feedback as well as positive reinforcement for the board or the chief executive, or to bring a successful chief executive's service to a graceful end, they are important tools for succession thinking.

The results of the *Daring to Lead 2006* survey found that 34 percent of nonprofit chief executives leaving their positions are either fired or otherwise forced out. It did not study the reasons. Some executive exits are precipitated by executives who act as lone rangers, push their own agendas, perpetually ignore or defy the board's actions, or worse. In other cases, the board can be the source of the problem. Conflicts with boards arising from individual board members who act as surrogate administrators, represent special interests, or undermine their executives also represent common and unstated reasons for chief executive job dissatisfaction and resignations. Some organizations have experienced high chief executive turnover because the board has either undergoverned or micromanaged. At other organizations, unfortunately, the board is clueless about management problems that have been filtered or suppressed until a crisis erupts.

Organizations with serial executive leadership transitions need to stop and ask themselves whether the governance model or the execution of the model impedes the retention of qualified leaders or turns off qualified candidates from applying for new searches. When executive turnover is high, the board should not be too quick to mount a search for the new chief executive until the source of the governance problem has been diagnosed and addressed by more than a symptomatic fix. When succession planning is continuous, remedies for problems or dysfunctional practices can be identified and often implemented in advance of the executive search phase of succession planning.

Executive compensation is now being scrutinized by regulators, Congress, and charity watchdog groups. As a result, all board members must understand the organization's executive compensation practices, not just those who serve on the executive or compensation committee. The revised IRS Tax Form 990, which took effect in 2008, contains questions regarding the way in which compensation has been determined for the chief executive and senior employees. To ensure that the organization will offer a competitive compensation package, the board should review national and regional nonprofit chief executive compensation surveys, make discreet phone calls to compare compensation levels with peer organizations of similar scope, and consider which non–salary components of the compensation package might offer a more competitive compensation package.

Nonprofit chief executive salary surveys are published by organizations such as the American Society of Association Executives (www.asaecenter.org), Abbott and Langer (www.abbott-langer.com), and the Council on Foundations (www.cof.org). WorldatWork (www.worldatwork.org), formerly the American Compensation Association, is an excellent source of information on survey sources. Umbrella organizations in your region such as your state nonprofit agency and local society of association executives can also be good sources of professional staff compensation and benefits levels. To find a list of state nonprofit associations, go to www.councilofnonprofits.org. For additional resources, guidelines, and issues related to chief executive compensation, benefits, and terms of employment see *Nonprofit Executive Compensation: Planning, Performance, and Pay, Second Edition,* by Brian Vogel and Charles W. Quatt (BoardSource, 2010).

At least once a year, boards should review not only the chief executive's salary, but also potential provisions that will contribute to a high performer's job satisfaction. Organizations that pay higher salaries are more likely to be able to supplement their leaders' salaries with benefit plans. Smaller organizations with tight resources often find creative ways to add other benefits consistent with the organization's values to accommodate their employees. All boards should ensure that the chief executive has an adequate amount of annual leave and insist that vacations be taken. The chief executive should be encouraged to participate in professional development opportunities that provide him or her with professional growth, a safe learning haven with peers and experts, and opportunities for renewal away from the organization.

While sabbaticals for chief executives are not the prevailing practice in nonprofit organizations (other than higher education and other large institutions), more organizations could probably find ways to cover the absence of a chief executive for a one- to three-month sabbatical after several years of service. Other ways to reduce the chances of burnout, stimulate personal renewal, and raise executive performance should be explored to give the chief executive regular opportunities to get away from the daily grind of the job.

Board support of the chief executive is especially important in times of conflict. The chief executive is often under siege when executing controversial policies the board has approved. This is not the time for the board to detach from the chief executive or the policy, but rather to help the executive manage the conflict. If the chief executive needs additional help in accomplishing a task, qualified consultants should be considered to assist with issues of organizational development, governance, management, and strategy. Once the decision has been made that an executive leadership transition is needed, the board should ensure that the strategic goals, priorities, and needs of the organization will inform the desired qualifications of the next chief executive rather than the other way around.

## Succession Planning Points to Remember

- Learn about the demands on the chief executive and the nature of the job.

- Develop an emergency leadership transition management plan.

- Clarify the mutual expectations between the chief executive and the board.

- Design and implement a constructive performance assessment process for the chief executive as well as a board self-assessment process.

- In setting the chief executive's compensation, ensure that the board has conducted itself in accordance with

  - bylaws

  - employment policies or contracts

  - good judgment

  - best practices

  - applicable state and federal laws and regulations

- Help create the conditions that will provide a climate for the chief executive to be an effective leader.

# CHAPTER 3

## DETERMINING WHERE THE ORGANIZATION WANTS TO GO PRIOR TO AN EXECUTIVE TRANSITION

The search for the new chief executive creates a pivotal inflection point for strategic, operational, and cultural changes that can either advance or impede progress. While succession planning does not start with the executive search process, it is essential that a board devote sustained and careful attention to this phase of the succession planning process. Too many chief executive job announcements describe the ideal, often heroic qualities required in the model chief executive without any evidence that they are based on a genuine institutional appraisal.

The competencies sought in the next chief executive must be adjusted to fit each organization's unique drivers of change and institutional needs. It should not be based on the strengths or deficiencies of the outgoing chief executive. The first step in any executive search is not the search for the new executive but a search for where the organization wants to go. One of the keys to a successful executive transition is a thoughtful process that begins when the board takes the time to understand the organization's current and future challenges, strengths, and needs.

Unfortunately, too many boards in quest of new chief executives start in the middle of the process, moving too quickly into the stage of identifying the qualities the ideal candidate should possess before defining strategic institutional issues and priorities. Successful succession planning enables the board to clarify the organization's strategic directions, the culture it aspires to sustain, and the kind of leadership that will advance its mission and vision prior to the search and selection process. This chapter describes the kinds of questions that the board should address when an executive transition is required.

This organizational assessment stage enables the board to gather the information needed to prepare a profile of the next chief executive and to determine if board members share a common view of the organization's priorities and directions. The best candidates will not demand unanimity from all board members on all issues, but they will be looking for evidence of organizational self-knowledge about critical issues, the results of past discussions on alternative futures, and areas prompting the most divergent points of view. While the format, content, and timing of the organizational assessment will depend on the needs and circumstances of your nonprofit, the process should include the following dimensions.

# SURVEY THE STAKEHOLDERS

Who should be involved in the organizational assessment process depends on the size, scope, and culture of the organization. It is a task that should be undertaken by the board as a whole in consultation with key constituencies, not by the search committee alone. The board has the ultimate responsibility for evaluating the present condition of the organization, the challenges looming on the horizon, and the future directions that will enable the organization to survive and grow.

But board members often have a more narrow view of how well the organization is functioning. This is because they typically have limited time to spend on their volunteer board commitments, they may not be as knowledgeable about the needs and desires of the organization's constituents, and they receive a good part of their information from the chief executive. While every board member should be invited to participate in this organizational self-examination, input from other key stakeholders is important. It can provide the board with a fresher and wider perspective from the viewpoint of key constituencies.

Staff members can provide valuable perspectives on the needs of the organization and the style of leadership required. Boards should provide safe forums for staff members, especially those who will report directly to the chief executive, to make candid suggestions on the organization's leadership needs and challenges. Other individuals, such as consumers or clients of the organization, the incumbent chief executive, major funders, direct service volunteer leaders, consultants who have worked with the organization in areas of strategy and organizational development, independent program and management evaluators, and key members can help respond to all or parts of the organizational assessment. This is also a good time to consult with respected outsiders who bring useful perspectives about the organization and its needs that the board should take into account in thinking about the next chief executive.

## ASSESS THE ORGANIZATION

Ideally, the board should take as long as it needs to undertake the organizational assessment well before it begins to look for chief executive candidates. If the organization has not engaged in a recent strategic thinking process (such as strategic planning or a review of the mission statement) and needs more time to conduct the institutional assessment, it is better to appoint an interim chief executive to enable the board to complete this process thoroughly than to jump into the search for candidates too quickly.

The organizational assessment process might begin with a survey and end with a retreat or workshop dedicated to reviewing the organizational objectives and priorities that emerge from the survey results. At some organizations, the results of such a survey have been incorporated into a draft organizational profile to be circulated to key stakeholders for review and comment before the chief executive profile is prepared.

While the results of recent strategic planning can provide a useful framework for an organizational assessment, it is neither required in advance of nor a substitute for an organizational assessment. The strategic priorities and underlying assumptions in the strategic plan may need to be revisited and updated. Organizations in the midst of strategic planning when an executive transition occurs will have to decide whether or not to defer strategic planning to allow the new chief executive to contribute to the results of such an important endeavor.

The precise method of organizational assessment is less critical than figuring out which questions will yield the best appraisal of the organization's present condition and its future needs. The objective here is not to evaluate every aspect of the internal and external operations of the organization, but to illuminate the salient institutional issues the next chief executive is expected to take on.

## ORGANIZATIONAL ASSESSMENT QUESTIONS THAT DETERMINE THE CONTEXT FOR UPCOMING CHIEF EXECUTIVE LEADERSHIP TRANSITIONS

The assessment tool should be reasonably simple in design and execution, and the process must be perceived as meaningful. Questions in these eight key areas provide examples of the kinds of issues and queries that are likely to yield common themes and perceptions regarding an organization's needs and directions:

| | |
|---|---|
| 1. Mission | 5. Management |
| 2. Vision | 6. Communications |
| 3. Financing | 7. Organizational culture |
| 4. Governance | 8. Additional questions |

See the sidebar "Two Organizational Evaluation Tools" on page 29 for a discussion of two organizational evaluation tools developed by BoardSource and the Drucker Foundation. They are offered as alternatives that could be used during this stage of the chief executive succession planning process. Boards and search committees should adapt and customize these existing organizational assessment tools and the following questions to meet the specific needs of the organizations they govern.

### 1. MISSION

A good place to start in the organizational assessment is to revisit the organization's reason for existence. If the mission statement does not serve as an up-to-date guidepost to planning and decision making, it may be best to wait until the new chief executive is in place to guide the organization through the delicate exercise of mission revision. This is a good time to invite questions that board members and other stakeholders may have regarding the organization's fundamental purpose and the drivers of change that the next chief executive must tackle. If there are significant philosophical differences about the organization's core purpose, this will impinge on the next chief executive's work.

Questions to Consider

- Is our current mission statement an adequate reflection of our organization's present reason for existence?

- Do the organization's programs, services, and products reflect our mission?

- What will be most important for our next chief executive to understand about our mission?

## 2. VISION

If mission is what the organization is, vision is what the organization strives to be. The view of the organization's desired future will help the board determine the kind of chief executive it needs to guide that vision. If current consensus on a clear, well-understood vision does not exist, it is better to say to the chief executive candidates, "Here are some of the key questions that we have about our future direction" or "We need to decide where the organization should go and what it should be over the next few years, and here are some of the choices we face."

In this case, a board might be looking not only for a leader who could help craft the long-range vision for the organization, but one who could design an inclusive process for engaging board, staff, and others in visionary thinking. Chief executive candidates often find it premature to answer the common interview question from board members, "What is your vision for this organization?" Search committees that ask interviewed candidates, "If you became the chief executive of this organization, how would you go about developing a vision for it?" are likely to learn a great deal more.

Questions to Consider

- Do we have a collective vision of what will be different three to five years from now as a result of the work of our organization?

- What are the principal accomplishments we want to produce during the next five years?

- How will we expect the next chief executive to help us define and create our preferred future? Are we looking for a visionary or a chief executive who will engage others in defining, refining, and responding to the organization's vision?

## 3. FINANCING

The board is ultimately responsible for the financial well-being of the organization. Ideally, a robust strategic plan linked to a realistic financial plan, adequate reserves, and sound financial controls are in place to attract the next chief executive. This is often not the case in the nonprofit sector. Heavy dependence on limited sources of revenue, declining income streams, and uncertainty about how to build future financial stability can create unrealistic expectations for securing a rainmaker chief executive. In other cases, the actual financial condition of the organization is either not clear to the board or not adequately revealed to the candidates. The organizational assessment stage is a good time for the board to make sure it has a true picture of whether the organization's financial condition is strong, weak, or steady.

Questions to Consider

- What are our major sources of revenue, and what proportion of our expenses do they support?

- Are our key revenue sources rising or falling?

- Do we have sufficient reserves?

- What expectations will we place on the next chief executive to generate new revenue, explore alternative revenues formulas, or employ other measures to create greater financial stability (e.g., raising funds from private sources, increasing dues from new members or membership categories, designing new programs or services sold to new members or customers)?

- Will the new chief executive be expected to help the board put better financial controls into place?

## 4. GOVERNANCE

The role, structure, and performance of the organization's board and how it views its relationship to the chief executive will influence the character of an executive leadership transition. The board is better positioned to understand this if there has been an assessment of the board's composition, structure, and core practices on an ongoing basis, as discussed earlier. Whether or not the board has engaged in regular assessment, it should take some time to define its role in relationship to the new chief executive, to identify areas of board operation that need attention, and to highlight how a new chief executive will be expected to work with and through the board.

In too many cases, discussions about governance deficiencies are deferred until the new chief executive starts the job. Telling the truth about dysfunctional governance cultures is often avoided because it exposes people to charges of bias and expectations of remedies. But if board members refuse to examine the underlying issues for chronically troublesome behaviors and practices, they will continue to breed for the new executive.

For example, if too many board members have been inappropriately functioning as surrogate administrators or representatives of special interests, if the board chair lacks the horsepower to work with a new chief executive, or if the board has delegated its stewardship to a board within the board, the organizational assessment phase is the time to diagnose the problem. This reduces the chances the next chief executive will inherit the board from hell. Failure to define and, if necessary, correct governance problems can shorten the new chief executive's term of service and launch another search much sooner than anticipated.

Questions to Consider

- How does the board add the greatest value to the organization at this time?

- Which areas of governance or board operation are in need of attention or improvement? What needs to change before the board hires the chief executive? How will it expect the next chief executive to help the board address these matters?

- How can the board and the next chief executive work most effectively together to build and maintain a strong working relationship?

- What kind of authority is the board prepared to grant the next chief executive, and what kind of accountability mechanisms should it consider to ensure responsible board oversight of the chief executive's performance?

- Does the current chief executive's job description need to be revised?

## 5. MANAGEMENT

Two of the most precious assets of most nonprofit organizations are the employees and volunteers who advance the organization's mission through day-to-day work. Unless the organization is largely volunteer driven, a major portion of the chief executive's time will be spent on hiring, overseeing, evaluating, empowering, and retaining the right staff. The human resource skills of the chief executive are likely to change as the organization evolves, particularly as the number of direct reports to the chief executive decrease as the staff grows. Nevertheless, everyone expects the chief executive to create a climate that fosters high performance, healthy group dynamics, and accountability from staff and volunteers. The members of the board, and especially the members of the professional staff, will be key sources of intelligence on the kind of management style that will work best.

Questions to Consider

- What are our greatest human resources challenges?

- What kind of management style does our organization need in the next chief executive to recruit, motivate, and retain the best and brightest staff members? Will this require a change from the current organizational culture?

- What behaviors in our next chief executive are likely to build trust, high performance, and accountability from our employees?

- What role will we expect our next chief executive to play in the management of our direct service volunteers?

## 6. COMMUNICATIONS

An increasingly competitive environment and greater scrutiny from government regulators, donors, members, and service recipients have prompted nonprofit leaders to invest greater resources in actively promoting the unique value of their services and activities. An executive leadership transition affords an opportunity to review how the next chief executive can strengthen the organization's marketing, public relations, promotion, and outreach efforts.

Questions to Consider

- What and who are the market(s) we serve and the people who decide whether to participate in or purchase our programs, services, or products?

- How well do we keep our members, clients, customers, donors, and other stakeholders informed about our work?

- How can our next chief executive help us design and implement more effective communications strategies?

- What role do we expect our next chief executive to play in our communications with our various constituents?

## 7. ORGANIZATIONAL CLUTURE

An organization's culture reflects the human side of organizational life — the written and unwritten rules that shape how it operates and the basic assumptions and shared beliefs about the place that people bring to their work. These values are often so ingrained in the life of the organization that they are unstated until the organization undertakes a formal process such as strategic planning, significant restructuring, or an executive leadership transition. During the organizational assessment stage, board members should determine which aspects of the communal culture need to be nurtured, altered, or radically changed. This will provide major clues for determining the skills and personal style the next chief executive must bring to accomplish this task.

Questions to Consider

- What are the core values, beliefs, or assumptions about how our organization operates that will be important for our next new chief executive to understand?

- Which values reflect "non-negotiable behaviors" that we want the chief executive to uphold and nurture?

- What creates the greatest frustration, confusion, or dysfunctional behavior in our organization that we will want the new chief executive to help us change?

- Will the chief executive need to fit the culture and traditions of our organization, or will he or she be expected to change it? How?

## 8. CHIEF EXECUTIVE LEADERSHIP QUESTIONS

Each organizational assessment questionnaire should include additional questions that do not fit neatly into the above categories but are likely to bear fruit for the chief executive profile.

Questions to Consider

- What are the mega issues facing the organization that should consume the greatest amount of the chief executive's time?

- What are the key drivers of change in the external and internal environment that we expect our chief executive to help us tackle?

- What must the chief executive do particularly well in order for the organization to fulfill its mission?

- Have we recently engaged in strategic planning? If so, how adequate is our current plan? If not, what kind of strategic thinking process do we want our next chief executive to help us launch?

- Are we looking primarily for continuity or change from our next chief executive?

- What are the top three leadership skills that we most need from our next chief executive?

- What personal qualities and relationship skills does our chief executive need to succeed?

- What behaviors and skills do we want our chief executive to model as a leader and a manager that are important in our organizational value system?

- What specific performance indicators will demonstrate that our chief executive is successful after his or her first three months?

- What suggestions do we have for the board to attract, recruit, and retain the most qualified candidate?

A board that undertakes the executive search process without assessing and articulating the organization's current issues and leadership needs is neglecting one of the most critical phases of succession planning. Boards that do not invest in an adequate organizational assessment before beginning the executive search phase frequently end up creating requirements for the new chief executive that are based solely on the perceived strengths or deficiencies of the last occupant of the office. This can also discourage qualified candidates from proceeding to the next level if it becomes clear from the halting responses to their questions that the board has not taken the time to genuinely explore organizational needs.

Each organization will have different needs and circumstances that affect the executive transition, but a confidential survey of key stakeholders can provide the search committee with unvarnished feedback on the strengths and challenges the next executive must tackle. When an organizational assessment is not done effectively, the search committee lacks critical context to match the needs of the organization with the skills and qualities needed in next chief executive. What emerges from an effective organizational assessment is a blueprint for the type of leadership needed to help initiate progress in the common, critical areas that are identified by survey respondents. The next chapter identifies ways for the board to identify leadership competencies and to address other key succession planning issues during the executive search phase of the succession planning process.

## TWO ORGANIZATIONAL EVALUATION TOOLS

These diagnostic tools can also be used or adapted to develop an organizational assessment during an executive leadership transition.

- *The Drucker Foundation Self-Assessment Tool for Nonprofit Organizations*

This self-assessment book, published by Jossey-Bass, is based on five questions related to Peter Drucker's central management principles: What is our business (mission)? Who is our customer? What does the customer consider value? What have been our results? What is our plan? It provides background, examples, and a number of worksheets designed to help nonprofit leaders think through each of the important questions for their organization and their role in it.

- *Navigating the Organizational Lifecycle: A Capacity-Building Guide for Nonprofit Leaders* by Paul M. Connolly (BoardSource, 2006)

The nonprofit organizational lifecycle assessment tool and strategies in this book will help board members and chief executives prepare for different kinds of passages such as executive transitions. The results of this assessment will help organizational leaders

- determine if capacities are properly aligned with the current stage of development

- identify weaknesses and situations that create change, growth, challenges, and opportunities

- illustrate how board composition and responsibilities may change as the organization evolves

- encourage boards to be more strategic and proactive in planning for the future

- consider the implications for what will be required in the next chief executive

## SUCCESSION PLANNING POINTS TO REMEMBER

- Begin an executive search by asking where the organization wants to go.

- Identify the right questions to ask that illuminate the institutional strengths, needs, and challenges that require executive leadership.

- Select the best diagnostic tool to execute an organizational assessment.

- Engage key stakeholders in assessing the needs of the organization as well as the leadership competencies required in the next chief executive.

# CHAPTER 4
## *SIX KEY ISSUES FOR THE BOARD TO ADDRESS DURING THE EXECUTIVE SEARCH*

### 1. DEFINE THE CORE LEADERSHIP AND MANAGEMENT COMPETENCIES

One of the board's most important succession-planning transactions will be to convert the results of the organizational assessment into a meaningful set of personal and professional competencies that match the organization's core needs. It can be argued that there are some qualities that every nonprofit chief executive will need — a commitment to the cause, stamina, judgment, strength of character, and a mastery of basic management skills in finance, human resources, communications, and administrative systems. If the right questions have been addressed during the organizational assessment phase, the emerging profile of the organization's current needs and where it must go creates a portrait for the kind of professional leadership required to help take it there.

To determine which leadership competencies are most essential to the organization's success, zero in on the strategic imperatives that emerge from the organizational assessment. Does it reveal that the organization most needs a visionary who can frame the strategy, drive innovation, and radically grow the organization? Or do the results of the assessment highlight a need for a seasoned manager who can provide stability and make fine-course corrections as needed? Will the organization need primarily a turnaround expert who can restructure and rehabilitate an organization in extremis? Or does it need a leader who can take a good organization to new heights by securing new financing and forging new alliances? Does the chief executive need to be a transformational change-agent who can navigate the turbulent passages required to keep the organization robust and responsive to dramatic changes in the market it serves? Or does he or she simply need to bring a sufficient reserve of adaptive skill, among other things, to promote stability during unpredictable times?

The tempting answer would be "All of the above!" in light of the broad repertoire of competencies most boards expect from today's nonprofit chief executive. But each strategic situation reflected in the above questions has implications for the leadership qualities best aligned with organizational needs and key tasks. Nonprofit organizations engaged in chief executive succession planning range in scope from small, fragile, volunteer-driven organizations to large, well-financed, complex institutions that operate globally. While most boards expect their organizations to be well led and well managed, the reality is that in larger organizations the same person may not fulfill all of these roles.

Few executives will be equally gifted in all of the leadership requirements that emerge from the organizational assessment. The goal is to develop a highly focused, relevant, and authentic list of qualifications connecting the organization's needs to the requirements of the chief executive — without simply parroting the theoretical leadership constructs on the usual list of suspects for the model chief executive.

## MANAGEMENT SKILLS OFTEN TRUMP LEADERSHIP COMPETENCIES

"For years, boards have hired for management skills over leadership skills. This trend has increasingly placed a premium on the ability to manage finances and fundraise over competencies that reflect whole-systems thinking, such as the ability to build shared vision and facilitate the ongoing engagement of multiple stakeholders toward that vision. Management skills are important, of course, but they aren't the drivers of true 'nonprofit excellence.'"

"Boards and Leadership Hires: How to Get It Right" by Deborah Linnell, *The Nonprofit Quarterly,* Spring 2008

There have been many studies of what makes leaders successful. Drawing on groundbreaking brain and behavioral research, Daniel Goleman, a behavioral science columnist with *The New York Times,* found that the qualities of outstanding leaders have less to do with either IQ or management prowess. These leaders demonstrate a set of "emotional-intelligence" characteristics that include self-awareness and impulse control, persistence, zeal and self-motivation, empathy, and social deftness.

The relative importance of the underlying characteristics that will distinguish outstanding performance will depend in part on the circumstances. The best chief executives are not so much clones of the generic competencies attributed to exceptional leaders as they are individuals who perform well as leaders as the situation demands. Once the board has taken the time to determine the organization's present condition and its future needs, the following four skill sets may provide some insights and potential language regarding the qualities to consider. They can be approached in different ways by a number of thoughtful leadership observers.

1. General leadership and management competencies

2. Strategic thinking competencies

3. Board competencies

4. People competencies

Many of the competencies that emerge from the organizational assessment phase are likely to fall under these four general categories. In other cases, entirely different skill sets may bubble up as either essential or desirable characteristics. Determining the kind of chief executive needed by the organization is the bridge between the organizational assessment and the creation of the chief executive profile during the executive search phase of succession planning.

## GENERAL LEADERSHIP AND MANAGEMENT COMPETENCIES

These days, chief executives are urged to come with expeditionary and experimental mindsets to respond to changing technologies, intensified competition, and unexpected market conditions in a complex, fast-changing environment. The personal attributes that many leadership experts and practitioners ascribe to successful chief executives relate to their capacity for long-range thinking, constructing pictures of the future, and navigating change. In fact, many search committees prepare what-if scenarios for interviews and reference calls. These scenarios are designed to probe candidates' abilities to dissect complex problems, draw upon multiple perspectives, and develop new strategies and tactics.

In *The Work of Leadership,* authors Ronald Heifetz and Donald Laurie use the helpful metaphor of "getting on the balcony" to describe the need for leaders who move back and forth between the playing field and the balcony to mobilize the people in an organization to do adaptive work. They note that leaders have to be able to view patterns from this perspective because "It does them no good to be swept up in the field of action. Leaders have to see a context for change or create one. They should give employees a strong sense of the history of the enterprise and what's good about its past, as well as an idea of the market forces at work today and the responsibility people must take in shaping the future. Leaders must be able to identify struggles over values and power, recognize patterns of work avoidance, and watch for the many other functional and dysfunctional reactions to change."

For most chief executives, management expertise is a necessary but insufficient requirement for the job. In his article, "What Leaders Do" (*Havard Business Review,* Dec. 2001) John Kotter argues that management and leadership are distinctly different functions, yet complementary and essential for the contemporary leader. Kotter asserts that management is about efficiency and effectiveness directed to key dimensions of complexity, such as the quality of programs. Leadership is about coping with change, setting a direction, and motivating people to embrace an alternative future.

A growing number of leadership and management experts dismiss the notion of a distinct leadership personality, style, or a uniform set of traits that can predict the success of a chief executive. In his foreword to *The Leader of the Future,* Peter Drucker wryly observes that the only common personality trait he has encountered in effective leaders is something they did not have: "they had little or no 'charisma' and little use either for the term or for what it signifies." Drucker shares the following common behaviors that he observed in a host of effective leaders with different styles and abilities:

- They did not start out with the question, "What do I want?" They started out asking, "What needs to be done?"

- They then asked, "What can and should I do to make a difference?" This has to be something that both needs to be done and fits the leader's strengths and the way she or he is most effective.

- They constantly asked, "What are the organization's mission and goals? What constitutes performance and results in this organization?"

- They were extremely tolerant of diversity in people and did not look for carbon copies of themselves. It rarely even occurred to them to ask, "Do I like or dislike this person?" But they were totally, fiendishly intolerant when it came to a person's performance, standards, and values.

- They were not afraid of strength in their associates. They gloried in it. Whether they had heard of it or not, their motto was what Andrew Carnegie wanted to have put on his tombstone: "Here lies a man who attracted better people into his service than he was himself."

- One way or another, they submitted themselves to the "mirror test" — that is, they made sure that the person they saw in the mirror in the morning was the kind of person they wanted to be, respect, and believe in. This way they fortified themselves against the leader's greatest temptations — to do things that are popular rather than right and to do petty, mean, sleazy things.

Source: *The Leader of the Future* by Frances Hesselbein; "Forward" by Peter Drucker. Jossey-Bass, 1996. Reprinted by permission of John Wiley & Sons, Inc.

## CHARACTERISTICS OF LEADERS OF HIGH-PERFORMING ORGANIZATIONS

In *Leading People*, author Robert Rosen discusses eight characteristics he has observed in chief executives of healthy, high-performing organizations.

1. Vision — Leaders see the whole picture and articulate that broad perspective with others. By doing so, leaders create a common purpose that mobilizes people and coordinates their efforts into a single, coherent, agile enterprise.

2. Trust — Without trust, vision becomes an empty slogan. Trust binds people together, creating a strong, resilient organization. To build trust, leaders are predictable, and they share information and power. This goal is a culture of candor.

3. Participation — The energy of an organization is the participation and effort of its people. The leader's challenge is to unleash and focus this energy, inspiring people at every level of the enterprise to pitch in with their minds and hearts.

4. Learning — Leaders need a deep understanding of themselves. They must know their strengths and shortcomings, which requires a lifelong process of discovery, and they must be able to adapt to new circumstances. So too with their organization. It must promote constant innovation, and the leaders must encourage their people to refresh their skills and renew their spirits.

5. Diversity — Successful leaders know the power of diversity and the poison of prejudice. They understand their own biases, and they actively cultivate an appreciation of the positive aspects of people's differences. In their organizations, they insist on a culture of mutual respect.

6. Creativity — In a world where smart solutions outpace excessive work, creativity is crucial. Leaders pay close attention to people's talents, leaning on their strengths and managing around their weaknesses. They encourage independent, challenging thinking, and they invest in technologies that facilitate the efforts of their people.

7. Integrity — A leader must stand for something. As a public citizen and a private person, he or she knows what is important in life and acts by deep-stated principles. Every wise leader has a moral compass, a sense of right and wrong. Good leaders understand that good ethics is good business.

8. Community — Community is mutual commitment, and it inspires the highest performance. It is human nature to go the extra mile for one's neighbors and fellow citizens, and a mature leader stresses the organization's responsibility to the surrounding society. A leader also acts as steward of the natural environment.

Reprinted by permission of Robert Rosen.

While leadership experts such as Peter Drucker and Robert Rosen suggest thoughtful language, each board must take the time to determine the distinctive values and actions that contribute most significantly to outstanding leadership and positive outcomes in the organization it governs. For example, some organizations may look for a deep, personal spirituality in addition to human interactive and analytic competencies. For other organizations, these leadership strengths may include experience with contemplative and reflective practices that are consistent with the organization's value system.

A number of desired leadership competencies will prove to be elusive, almost indescribable, and even more difficult to discern in candidates through interviews or reference calls. For example, if it is important to create a culture of inquiry, how does the board assess the candidates' tolerance for candor, divergent viewpoints, and even dissent within the organization? Difficulty in articulating important leadership competencies should not preclude the board from addressing them with the candidates chosen for interviews.

## STRATEGIC THINKING COMPETENCIES

The traditional top-down, upper-management–driven approach of adopting a three- to five-year strategic plan with fixed strategies is becoming obsolete. This politburo planning style is being replaced with shorter cycles and decentralized, consultative practices that enlist a wide range of stakeholders in the planning process. Metrics, timelines, and scheduled reviews are being added once the plan is developed to enable the board and staff to continuously revisit the plan to track progress, review underlying assumptions, and make midcourse corrections as needed. As a result, more nonprofit boards expect their chief executives to model and cultivate continuous strategic thinking.

Unfortunately, crafting institutional strategy is not a skill that is automatically acquired from management experience. When the chief executive does not come equipped with the capacity to think in big-picture terms or help the organization define its collective vision and strategic directions, this critical task tends to be cast aside for the day-to-day grind or delegated by default to others lacking sufficient institutional perspective.

Boards should expect their executives to frame issues in a way that will allow the board to aim its sights on the issues that will make the greatest difference on the organization's capacity to advance its mission. When no compelling, overall strategy exists, the danger is that organizational resources will be channeled into the immediate and urgent rather than into those issues with the greatest stakes for the organization. When there is no destination or road map for where the organization is headed, the board is more likely to either micromanage or fall asleep at the switch. Just as individual board members can engage in micromanaging, chief executives can be guilty of undermanaging their responsibility to provide the board (and the staff) with the organizational framework and strategic priorities to guide its work.

## THE CHIEF EXECUTIVE AS BROKER

Studies of effective leaders often highlight the chief executive's ability to elicit and inspire the thinking of others in a shared vision for the organization. According to *Governing for Growth: Using 7 Measures of Success to Strengthen Board Dialogue and Decision Making,* one of the things that distinguishes remarkable nonprofit organizations from the comparison group is that the chief executive plays a key role in vision — not by imposing his or her personal vision but by facilitating visionary thinking throughout the organization.

The *7 Measures* research found that in remarkable associations, the chief executive

- operates as a broker of ideas

- engages others in defining, refining, and responding to the organization's vision

- listens and is open to others' ideas

- stimulates energy and fosters effective communication, engagement, and collaborative action among and between staff and volunteers

- is willing to step aside at times to facilitate a discussion of ideas without dictating an outcome

- helps both elected leaders and staff think in terms of what is possible

- enables things to happen rather than decreeing what will happen

*Governing for Growth: Using 7 Measures of Success to Strengthen Board Dialogue and Decision Making* by Nancy R. Axelrod. ASAE & The Center for Association Leadership, Washington, DC, 2009.

## Board Competencies

It would be hard to overstate how much the chief executive and the board will influence the quality and effectiveness of one another. A key challenge for many chief executives is how to provide strong leadership (that the board often invites at the time that a new chief executive is selected) without preempting and overshadowing the board. A key challenge for board members is how to be active, critical participants in matters of policy and strategy without micromanaging or circumventing the chief executive. These are the kinds of core governance dilemmas confronted by virtually all nonprofits in every mission area.

Research conducted by Bob Herman and Dick Heimovics in the early 1990s found that especially effective nonprofit executives differed most from their counterparts by the leadership behaviors directed to their boards. In *Executive Leadership in Nonprofit Organizations,* Herman and Heimovics indicate that successful chief executives facilitate interaction both within the board and between themselves and the board by

- attending to board members' feelings and needs

- envisioning changes in organizational functioning

- promoting and reinforcing board accomplishments

- providing useful decision-making information to the board

These kinds of board competencies require chief executives to come to their new positions with subtle and specialized group-dynamics skills that may be different from working with other types of groups. For example, nonprofit boards are often compared to symphony orchestras because the members must work together, depend on good leadership, and practice. But unlike professional musicians in a symphony orchestra, individual board members typically do not bring years of specialized board member training to their performance, they rarely study for their role, and their practice time as a collective board is sharply limited. Furthermore, many of the individuals who are selected for board service have had successful professional or volunteer careers with a greater parallel to the roles of conductors, composers, or solo performers than to team musicians.

Many nonprofit leaders yearn for their board members to bring a greater portion of their expertise to the boardroom than they actually do. But this yearning will not be fulfilled by exhortation. If chief executives are not willing to play an active role in creating the kinds of boards that provide the intellectual capital (as well as the fiduciary oversight) they claim they want, they are baying at the moon.

The way the chief executive and board chair use the board's time at board meetings will also influence the board's performance. The tools that are provided to the board can either foster or impede its capacity to provide insight as well as oversight. In order to help the board understand and act on what matters most to the long-term future of the organization, it is not enough for the chief executive to frame issues of policy and strategy. He or she must invite the board to weigh in on strategic objectives and priorities. For some organizations, this is bound to be a departure from the mind-numbing, dog-and-pony shows that pass for board meetings.

Once a board completes an honest appraisal of the mutual expectations between the chief executive and the board, it is better equipped to identify the board competencies it genuinely wants from the next chief executive. Let's pause briefly for a reality check — some chief executives prefer the steady sound of snoring or rubber stamping in the boardroom. Some board members view their executives as clerks rather than as colleagues and primary educators of the board. For nonprofit leaders with these values, the goal of a strong, interdependent board–chief executive partnership is largely illusory.

If the board does indeed expect the chief executive to play a significant role in helping it to be effective, a track record as a "board-centered executive" would be an excellent measure of a candidate's commitment to this process. If candidates with other desirable qualities have no demonstrable experience in this realm, these are skills that can be learned — but only if the prospective chief executive genuinely views the board as a strategic asset and is committed to enlisting the board as such. As discussed earlier, the success of the chief executive in building an effective board will depend on the board directing some comparable effort to the chief executive.

## "PEOPLE" COMPETENCIES

Robert Rosen observes that the best leaders allocate a good portion of their time to leading people because they "see themselves as the Chief People Officers of their enterprise." Unfortunately, some chief executives with apparently high intelligence, multiple professional skills, and management experience can and do perform poorly in the workplace.

Board members recognize that good interpersonal skills are not automatically linked to intelligence and experience, but they are often unsure of how to define these qualities or describe them in a chief executive profile for a variety of reasons. The board may be less likely to understand or agree on the noncognitive competencies needed for the job, or to assume that these traits will simply reveal themselves during the candidate interviews or reference calls. When the dimensions of the organization's culture are not clearly profiled in the results of the institutional assessment, it is even more difficult to reach consensus on the required people competencies.

Marcus Buckingham, an analyst for a Gallup poll that found that most workers rate having a caring boss even higher than money or fringe benefits, observes that "people join organizations and leave managers." In spite of the nobility of the cause that attracts so many of us to our work, this phenomenon occurs just as frequently in the nonprofit sector. Boards that take the time to articulate the discrete interpersonal skills their chief executives need related to communication, self-awareness, sensitivity, empathy, and proficiency in maintaining relationships are in a better position to actually find chief executives who possess them.

In 1990, John D. Mayer and Peter Salovey coined the term "emotional intelligence" to describe "a form of social intelligence that involves the ability to monitor one's own and others' feelings and emotions, to discriminate among them, and to use this information to guide one's thinking and actions." This term has now moved into the mainstream with research conducted by Daniel Goleman to capture something more complex than "being nice." One of Goleman's books is cited in the Suggested Resources section because of its potential value in identifying both the personal and social skills that are likely to affect chief executive performance as well as the costs of emotional illiteracy on organizations that do not have leaders with these skills.

## 2. CREATE THE CHIEF EXECUTIVE PROFILE

Matching the needs of the organization with the leadership competencies sought in the next chief executive is one of the board's most important transactions in the executive search phase of the succession planning process. The chief executive profile refers to the final document approved by the board before the job is announced. It describes

- the organization and its needs

- the principal responsibilities of the next chief executive

- the required leadership competencies

- the desired experience and qualifications of the candidates

- the compensation

- the procedures for applying or nominating candidates

The litmus test for the chief executive profile is how authentically and concretely it links the genuine values and needs of the organization with the behaviors and competencies needed in the next chief executive. John Gardner once noted, "The identifying of values is a light preliminary exercise before the real and heroic task, which is to make the values live.... Moral, ethical, or spiritual values come alive only when living men and women recreate the values for their time — by living the faith, by caring, by doing. It is true of religion; it is true of democracy; it is true of personal ethical codes." It is also true of chief executive profiles and leadership transitions.

If a search committee is taking the responsibility to draft the chief executive profile, it should not get too far out ahead of the board in the search process. Engaging each member of the board in the institutional assessment stage and asking the board to approve the final chief executive profile before it is announced and shared publicly are two practices that will help minimize this danger. A sample chief executive profile for a fictional organization can be found in Appendix 2.

## 3. CONSIDER HIRING AN INTERIM CHIEF EXECUTIVE

It's also important to explore the merits of hiring an interim chief executive to bridge the leadership gap between the departure of the incumbent and the start date of a successor. A growing number of organizations now hire either an acting executive from within the organization or an interim chief executive who does not serve on the board or staff. This interim leadership can give the board sufficient time to determine what the organization needs in its next executive, to conduct a thorough search, or to help the organization address key issues that need attention before qualified candidates can be recruited.

For organizations that have not engaged in continuous succession planning, it is becoming more common to hire interim executives or acting chief executives to lay the groundwork for a successful executive transition. To pave the way for the next executive, interim chief executives can provide continuity in management during what is often an extended period of great uncertainty. A growing supply of seasoned professionals is becoming available to serve in this capacity. Some organizations project when and for how long they will hire an interim chief executive (in their succession plans or emergency leadership transition plans) while others wait until the conditions surrounding the executive transition are known.

### WHEN TO CONSIDER AN INTERIM CHIEF EXECUTIVE

Robert T. Van Hook, president of Transition Management Consulting, offers the following 10 potential scenarios for turning to a professional interim chief executive with the leadership and management skills to address these conditions:

1. The departure of the executive was sudden or tumultuous, and the board wants to get the organization back on an even keel before bringing on a new chief executive.

2. The board may feel that the organization is in pretty good operational shape, but it would like an outside review of its operations and governance to help refine the executive search.

3. The organization may have serious operational problems that need to be stabilized or turned around before the permanent executive is hired, especially if the recruitment process is likely to be long.

4. The staff may be in a dysfunctional emotional state due to the sudden departure of the executive.

5. The organization may have or anticipate staff unrest and issues that an interim chief executive can help manage and resolve before the new executive arrives.

6. The organization may want to keep up the momentum needed during a period of rapid growth while the search process is underway.

7. The organization may have big events or initiatives planned that can't wait for the completion of the recruitment process but require the experience and skill of a professional interim chief executive.

8. There might not be an individual on staff with the experience and skill to manage the organization.

9. Staff members who may be qualified to perform at the interim chief executive job may not be able to add these responsibilities to their current portfolio.

10. The board may wish to allow current staff members to apply for the chief executive position without the perceived bias that may come with a staff member who is perceived as "heir apparent" or who would be highly disappointed if he or she does not get the job after serving as interim chief executive.

Reprinted by permission of Robert T. Van Hook.

This is also the time to consider if the organization can use help from consultants who specialize in organizational development, management, and governance matters. For example, some organizations invite consultants to help design and administer the organizational assessment survey, address human resources issues that need to be clarified or resolved, or assist the board in addressing specific governance problems that could be obstacles to recruiting and retaining qualified chief executive candidates. Whether the departure of the chief executive is sudden and traumatic or anticipated well in advance, the board should determine if it needs to hire an executive search consultant.

## HOW EXECUTIVE SEARCH CONSULTANTS ADD VALUE

The best executive search consultants will bring experience, knowledge of the nonprofit sector and mission area of the organization, good judgment, and dedicated time to devote to the executive search process. A number of boards choose to retain search consultants when the following things happen:

- The board wants to aggressively seek nominations for and recruit applicants from a diverse pool of the most qualified candidates rather than mount a recruitment process that relies primarily on responses to the mailed job announcement and advertisements about the position. (Some of the most qualified candidates are less likely to apply for the position because they are satisfied in their current jobs.)

- The search committee needs help in screening applicants and nominees to restrict board members' time to reviewing or interviewing the most qualified candidates.

- The search committee does not have the expertise to do a thorough and skillful job structuring the interview process for candidates or checking references in a manner that will yield candid feedback.

- A skilled third party is needed to help negotiate the terms of employment for the final candidates(s) in a manner that will satisfy the needs of both the finalist(s) and the organization.

## 4. DEVELOP A COMMUNICATIONS PLAN

A foundation of the executive transition phase of succession planning is process transparency — communicating the how and why of decisions in a timely way. Considerable uncertainty and anxiety mark leadership transition periods. Board and staff relationships can become dysfunctional. Staff members are understandably uneasy about what is going to happen when the new executive arrives. Staff members and other stakeholders should not have to interpret puffs of white smoke from the board to figure out what is happening.

To keep people engaged in and informed about what steps are being taken to find the right chief executive, it is helpful to provide opportunities for plenty of input from staff and other stakeholders in the process. The search committee chair should keep the entire board apprised of exactly where the committee is in its deliberations and what challenges, opportunities, and pitfalls it has encountered. The board should determine who the official spokesperson will be on the status of the search to reduce the chances that unfounded rumors, special interests, or confidential information will distort the message and undermine the search process.

It is critical to keep the entire community up to date on the status of the transition process during the several months that it usually takes from the announced departure of the incumbent to the start date of the new chief executive. Key constituencies to include in the communications loop might include funders, members, and local press, in addition to staff members. It is better to err on the side of providing too much information too frequently than the reverse. Announcements on Web sites, newsletter articles, special bulletins, customized letters, and phone calls can be especially timely at the following points:

- To announce why the chief executive is departing, provide statistics about the individual's term of service, and highlight his or her accomplishments

- To announce the formation of the search committee and its projected schedule

- To widely circulate the chief executive profile once it is developed by the search committee to encourage applicants and nominations

- To provide follow-up communication after the position has been announced that will keep people informed of the status of the search up until the time the chief executive has been chosen by the board

- To formally announce the appointment of the new chief executive to the entire community, including the local and professional media

- To share relevant information about the chief executive's observations, participation in special events, or key initiatives in the initial months of office

Executive searches almost always take longer than expected. During this time, people are likely to feel both excitement and fear about the emerging possibilities. The board and the search committee should not be so carried away with their work that they neglect to provide regular, timely, and meaningful updates to all stakeholders on decisions that have been made, as well as decisions that have not yet been made. Regular reporting and as much openness as possible (without violating the need to keep the names of candidates and other matters confidential) are essential to sustain faith in the integrity of the leadership transition process.

## 5. DEFINE THE ROLE OF THE OUTGOING CHIEF EXECUTIVE IN SUCCESSION PLANNING

Ultimately, the chief executive's most important contribution to succession planning is to build organizational capacity that will leave the organization stronger and better for his or her successor. Building a successful organization, demonstrating mission performance and impact, creating financial sustainability, and fostering an adaptive and accountable culture will increase the probability of a successful transition.

It is not the chief executive's job to anoint his or her successor. A concrete way for a chief executive to contribute to succession planning is to build organizational bench strength by nurturing staff members with leadership potential to advance within the organization. These professionals can become potential successors that the board may (or may not) choose to consider as qualified candidates. Whether or not these professionals become internal candidates or potential leaders for other organizations, they are likely to be a part of the management team that must continue to perform during an executive leadership transition. As a result, boards should be assessing their chief executives, in part, on how well they are developing opportunities and pathways for emerging leaders to advance within their organizations.

The reluctance on the part of many chief executives and board members to address succession planning with their boards may be comparable to the person who feels he just won't die if he does not prepare a will. But many thoughtful chief executives understandably struggle with how to address succession planning for fear of alarming their boards or causing them to overreact. Chief executives can contribute to succession planning by bringing up the issue with their boards well before an executive transition is likely to take place.

### RECOMMENDATIONS TO CHIEF EXECUTIVES ON EXECUTIVE LEADERSHIP TRANSITIONS

- Take responsibility for the board.
- Build a "leaderful organization" as a succession planning strategy.
- Ask for adequate salary and benefits.
- Ask for help.
- Pursue leadership development funding.
- Live in the question: Am I still the right person for this job?
- Engage in career planning.

*Daring to Lead 2006: A National Study of Nonprofit Executive Leadership.*

The optimum role for outgoing executives in the actual search process will depend on the circumstances surrounding their departure. For chief executives who have been terminated by the board for mismanagement, nonmanagement, or malfeasance, it is likely to be inappropriate for them to participate in any manner. While the chief executive should not be in charge of the succession planning process, he or she can participate in a number of ways. When the departure is voluntary, amicable, or planned, the departing chief executives who serve as the best role models often observe the following rules of engagement:

- Be available at the board's request to share insights about the organization's present condition and its future needs.

- Be willing to respond to final candidates who wish to speak with the last occupant of the office.

- Discourage individual staff, board members, and others from coming to you to vent accumulated gripes about the search process.

- If you are asked to play a role or execute a short-term assignment after your successor has been appointed, consult with the new chief executive for approval and guidance.

- Be supportive of the new leader.

- Whenever in doubt about how to participate in the executive transition in an appropriate manner, put the organization first by asking, "What role or response on my part would be in the best interests of the organization?"

Once the new executive or interim executive is chosen, the circumstances will dictate the best role for the outgoing chief executive. Perhaps the best thing the departing executive can do is to get out of the way. At one organization that hired an interim executive director, the outgoing chief executive took the following deliberate steps in the week remaining before his departure. He moved out of his office and announced to the board and staff that he was no longer making decisions for the organization. At a staff meeting, the staff and interim chief executive staged a light-hearted, effective ceremony of passing the leadership torch. This enabled the staff to begin to think positively about the transition because they and the departing executive had found a constructive way to bring closure to his tenure.

# 6. AVOID FIVE COMMON PITFALLS DURING THE EXECUTIVE SEARCH

1. During the negotiations stage of the selection process, boards and final candidates often dwell on matters of compensation and neglect to agree in advance on equally important issues. The latter include the terms of severance if the chief executive leaves for reasons other than for cause and the manner in which the executive's performance is to be evaluated.

2. While many search committees claim that mission experience can be more easily acquired than leadership skills, they are often too quick to reject candidates who do not come from the subsector in which the organization operates. This may unnecessarily diminish the supply of candidates who possess the necessary leadership and management skills, a keen interest in the cause, and a demonstrated track record of grasping new terrain quickly and deeply.

3. A common and dangerous bias that can undermine the selection process is when board members do not seek adequate information from a wide range of references after they fall in love with a candidate(s). Chemistry between the board and the chief executive is important, but it should not be the sole criterion or measured strictly by the candidates' performance during the relatively brief interviews.

4. When candidates include members of the staff or board, this can produce clumsy behavior that can be avoided with good practice. When this situation is not handled properly, it can be exceptionally tough on the internal candidate and the new chief executive, damage individual reputations and future careers, and imperil the transition process. Board members who wish to put their hat in the ring should resign from the board while they are being considered as active candidates to avoid conflict of interest. In general, both board members and staff members who are candidates should not be provided with information about the transition process that is not provided to the other candidates.

5. A number of new chief executives have discovered vital information that the search committee and the board did not disclose to the final candidate. The search committee and the board should follow the doctrine of "no surprises" in sharing information about the organization's strengths, weaknesses, financial condition, and its prospects before the chief executive is appointed. Both the quality of information and the manner in which it is shared will be revealing indicators to candidates about the nature of the organization and the character of the board. In addition to questions about mission and vision, final candidates will request and be entitled to receive more detailed information on the organization's financials, programs and services, future plans, and other governance and management documents.

## Working with Internal Candidates

To help the board, internal candidate(s), and the new chief executive plan good practices regarding the treatment of internal candidates, executive search consultant Larry Slesinger offers the following recommendations for the three key parties in this transaction:

Recommendations for the board:

- Find out right away if there will be any internal candidates.

- Do a search even if the internal candidate is exceptionally strong.

- Have an immediate conversation with the internal candidate even if the search committee is not yet ready to interview candidates.

- Put the internal candidate through all the steps you require of all other candidates.

- If the internal candidate is no longer being considered, tell him or her.

- If you choose someone else to be chief executive, tell the internal candidate before others.

Recommendations for the internal candidate:

- Realize that you probably will not get the job.

- If you are in a very senior position and you do not get the chief executive job, you should expect to leave the organization within 18 months.

- If you do not get the job, do not conclude that you are damaged goods. You're not — unless you start acting that way. (One of the most important things you can do is to give the new chief executive your full support beginning on the first day, without reservation or hesitation.)

Recommendations for the new chief executive:

- Meet the internal candidate before you meet the rest of the staff.

- Understand the role the internal candidate had at the organization, and be sensitive to ways that role will change under you.

- Learn from this person, especially since it's likely that he or she will leave and you will no longer be able to tap his or her knowledge.

- If the internal candidate decides to leave, offer your support.

Reprinted by permission of Larry Slesinger.

## SUCCESSION PLANNING POINTS TO REMEMBER

- Use the results of the organizational assessment to define the core leadership and management competencies needed in the next chief executive.

- Create a chief executive profile that links the values and needs of the organization with the competencies and behaviors needed in the next chief executive.

- Determine whether interim executive leadership is needed during the search.

- Develop and implement a communications plan that keeps appropriate stakeholders informed about the status of the search and engaged where appropriate.

- Help engage the outgoing chief executive in the search process in a meaningful way that is appropriate to the circumstances surrounding his or her departure.

- Avoid common pitfalls such as selecting the chief executive based solely on the results of the interview process.

# CHAPTER 5

## HIRING THE CHIEF EXECUTIVE DOES NOT COMPLETE THE SUCCESSION PLANNING PROCESS

The best executive leadership transition plans anticipate that the process does not end on the start date of the new chief executive. Yet it is quite common for boards to breathe a collective sigh of relief, congratulate all for the completion of a critical board task, and conclude that the last hurdle in the leadership transition has been overcome once the public announcement of the appointment has been made. Exaltation is understandable, but now begins another delicate stage of the succession planning process.

Board members deeply engaged in the transitional duties they took on before the new chief executive assumes office may have trouble relinquishing responsibilities they acquired to bridge a power vacuum. At the other extreme, too many boards detach too abruptly and completely from the leadership transition process. The heady combination of exhaustion and euphoria many board members feel at the end of a search is understandable. So is the desire to give the new executive some time to ease into the job. But irrational exuberance and detachment can result in an executive term that is shorter than the executive search process.

The chief executive's performance (and retention) will be influenced by the role of the board, the staff, and the incoming chief executive at the front end of the executive's tenure. This is a time that will require a skillful blend of board oversight and support without micromanagement, the chief executive's initiative in inviting and welcoming assistance, and, hopefully, the staff's proactive role in helping the new executive learn about the organization.

The following examples describe post-appointment leadership transition strategies that have been successfully implemented by real organizations for the express purpose of helping new executives succeed during their first 12 to 18 months of service.

## CONSIDER A LEADERSHIP TRANSITION TEAM

Before the board of a national nonprofit organization with regional offices around the country announced the appointment of the new chief executive, it established a transition team composed of the members of the search committee and four staff members.

The primary goals of the transition team were

- to support the organization (its staff, board, and new chief executive) through a successful transition

- to create the conditions for a leadership transition to occur in a manner healthy for the organization and its people

- to provide a feedback mechanism that assigned each individual staff and board member on the transition team the role of inviting and receiving comments and suggestions on the effectiveness of the transition

The projected activities included monthly meetings among the board chairman, the new chief executive, and the transition team; regular meetings in the national office with the new chief executive; regular conference calls with the new chief executive, regional, and local staff; and written monthly reports from the transition team to all board and staff members to keep them informed of leadership transition issues and events.

The common understandings of the transition team were that each member was expected to serve as a liaison to specific stakeholders within the organization throughout the transition; a communications plan would be developed to introduce the new chief executive to the organization's many publics (e.g., staff, volunteers, contractors, partner organizations); a national forum would take place within the executive's first eight months to bring all staff and board members and key direct service volunteers from 50 states together to meet her, revisit institutional goals, and share best practices; and a leadership transition consultant(s) would be used to help plan the national forum, shape and execute the organization's communications plan, and assist the new chief executive with key activities such as strengthening the institution's fundraising strategy.

## PROVIDE A FORMAL ORIENTATION PROGRAM FOR THE CHIEF EXECUTIVE

Unless the new executive has worked with the organization in some former capacity, he or she will have much to learn about new responsibilities, key players in the organization, and a variety of strategic and tactical issues that demand immediate attention. Ideally, both the board and the executive will actively participate in this process. At some organizations, an individual board or staff member, or both, will take on the early responsibility of sharing basic institutional information, addressing questions, and describing challenges. At others, members of the search committee, a new transition team, or a welcoming committee plan special events to formally introduce the new executive to key constituents, provide orientation on the organization and its culture, and act as transition guides as needed.

## POSITIONING THE NEW CHIEF EXECUTIVE FOR SUCCESS

The following practices helped the board, the new chief executive, and the staff of a national nonprofit association to focus on the same issues, develop clear expectations, and provide a basis for performance evaluation during the first few months of the chief executive's tenure:

- The chief executive met on a regular basis with the board chair to discuss priorities for the association and asked staff to provide her with information to better understand the organization, its priorities, and its culture.

- The chief executive had hour-long telephone calls with each board committee and association task force chair to better understand priorities.

- The chief executive developed in consultation with the board chair and her senior staff a work plan with priorities for the first six months.

- The chief executive shared the work plan with the board officers first and then the board for comments.

- The chief executive regularly discussed goals and priorities with the board chair.

- A six-month chief executive performance evaluation was conducted that was based primarily on the chief executive's update on work plan progress, the chief executive's job description, and her self-assessment.

- Prior to the board chair's report on the chief executive's performance to the board in executive session, the board chair met with the chief executive to share oral and written comments on her performance, using a chief executive self-assessment instrument and taking into consideration comments from board members and senior staff members who completed a different assessment instrument.

- After the six-month assessment, the chief executive and the board established a work plan that she shared with the board for comment.

- The chief executive encouraged the board to continue to give her feedback on her performance before the annual performance review scheduled at the end of her first year.

- The chief executive met at least monthly by conference call with the board officers to share her key activities, ask questions about key membership issues, and invite feedback from the board's leaders.

During this chief executive's first 10 months in office, two other initiatives made an enormous difference in creating a collective vision and mutual expectations among the board members, the chief executive, and the staff. The new chief executive, the board, and the staff allocated time to a strategic planning process that produced a new mission statement, a list of strategic priorities, a tactical plan, and key performance measures to be tracked and revisited at subsequent board and staff meetings. Second, the chief executive planned a staff retreat (in consultation with a staff planning committee and a consultant who facilitated the retreat) to determine how the staff could best contribute to the strategic plan, enhance communications, and work together most effectively as a team under the new administration.

## ENCOURAGE THE NEW CHIEF EXECUTIVE TO CONDUCT INFORMATIONAL INTERVIEWS

Both the new executive and the early transition team should take time to identify what kind of information the executive needs. One of the most valuable things a new executive can do is to listen to a variety of constituencies, and particularly to board and staff members. Many executives dedicate time early in their administrations to conduct individual interviews with their current and departing board and staff members (and other key stakeholders). The objective is to get a variety of perspectives on institutional strengths, weaknesses, opportunities, and challenges. If the former chief executive can serve as a useful resource, it works better when the new chief executive initiates this dialogue rather than the other way around.

The following interview questions can yield helpful information.

To ask individual staff members:

- Why do you choose to work here?

- What would you most like to contribute?

- What two or three things would you most like to change?

- What are the office "traditions" I should be aware of?

- What advice do you have on how I can work most effectively with the staff, the board, and other key constituents?

To ask individual board members:

- Why do you choose to serve on this board?

- How do you think this board adds the greatest value?

- Where do you think you can make the greatest difference as a board member?

- What are the issues that should command the greatest amount of board time during the next year?

- What advice do you have on how I can work most effectively with the board?

To ask board members who have recently completed their terms:

- Now that you have completed your term, what are the most valuable lessons you have learned about governance and the organization in general?

- What are the most important issues that the board addressed during your term of office?

- What were the board's greatest successes and mistakes during your term of office?

- Do you feel that you were able to make a difference as an individual board member?

- What advice would you give me on how I can work most effectively with the board?

- What concerns you most about the future of this organization?

## AGREE ON WRITTEN GOALS AND EXPECTATIONS FOR THE CHIEF EXECUTIVE

The new executive will bring a different style that can be received by others as a breath of fresh air or an ill wind. As board members monitor the climate during the chief executive's first few months, they should try to keep in perspective the many speed bumps likely to be encountered as a result of a change on this scale. Just about any departure from the status quo is likely to be greeted with critical scrutiny, if not active resistance, by some. These changes might include the grieving that often follows the departure of a revered former chief executive, personnel changes the new executive wants to make to build his or her own team, or a reorganization of units and systems.

Most boards view the selection of the new chief executive as a transformative act that will result in a multiyear term of office. Occasionally it turns out to be a briefer term of service than anticipated. In some instances, the tenure of the new executive is disconcertingly short because the board finds that the chief executive "was not the right fit." In other cases, board unrest and chief executive discomfort can simmer below the surface for some time until it erupts in a manner that requires a formal intervention. Until that time, board members and chief executives may make poor decisions because of their reluctance to define the problem, challenge each other's assumptions, and clarify expectations.

Many nonprofit boards and chief executives mistakenly assume that existing documents such as the mission statement, the chief executive's job description, the chief executive profile, or the strategic plan adequately define collective expectations. While new executives deserve some time to understand the terrain before committing to a plan of action, the board and the executive should work together as early as possible and as often as needed to agree on goals for the organization, define their respective roles, and decide which tasks require immediate, short-term, or long-term action. These early months are an important time for board members and executives to share their perceptions about how things are going, to celebrate achievements, and to work on problems before they fester.

Clearly, this process of defining mutual expectations between the board and the chief executive should relate to particular institutional circumstances, timing issues, and individual styles present in each particular leadership transition. Everyone who worked on the executive search needs some time to breathe once the appointment has been made. But the process of preparing written goals and expectations should not be deferred until it starts to become evident that board members and the chief executive are moving on different tracks.

This is not a one-way street. During these early months, the chief executive should be proactively seeking the board's advice and feedback and its active engagement in the governance process. The board, on the other hand, needs to determine the best way to help assimilate its new chief executive, embrace his or her strengths, and provide support in critical areas where he or she may lack experience or interest. Much of the responsibility for taking the initiative and working out the details will rest on the shoulders of the board chair and the chief executive who, one can only hope, will be up to the task.

## WHAT ARE THE CHARACTERISTICS OF AN EFFECTIVE WRITTEN STATEMENT OF MUTUAL EXPECTATIONS?

- It is developed because both the board and the chief executive believe it adds value.

- It reflects agreement by the chief executive and the board collectively on the organizational issues that will most demand the chief executive's time and attention.

- It is specific on issues and actions and realistic in its time frame.

- It carefully defines ambiguous leadership and management language such as "vision" or "expanding markets" to ensure that the board and chief executive interpret such terms in the same way.

- It is deployed as a means of enhancing communication between the board and the chief executive.

- While either the chief executive or a board officer might prepare the initial draft, the final statement should be reviewed and approved by the board and the chief executive.

- It is regularly reviewed along with other relevant documents at the time of the chief executive's performance assessment, the board self-assessment, and related occasions, and updated as necessary.

## CONSIDER AN EXECUTIVE COACH FOR THE NEW CHIEF EXECUTIVE

During his first several months on the job, the new chief executive of a large national organization began to tackle changes relating to the organization's financing, programs, and management practices that the board had encouraged him to make when he was hired. What he was less prepared to handle was the resistance to change that he encountered. The staff members and volunteers were not only encountering a new change agent but also a leader with a distinctly different style than his long-serving, well-liked predecessor. As part of the chief executive's and the board's commitment to his self-improvement as a leader, an executive coach was retained in the following manner.

The coach met individually with the chief executive's direct reports, board members, peers, and select staff and consultants. The purpose of the personal interviews was to provide the coach with specific, timely, and actionable feedback regarding their perceptions of the executive's strengths and areas for development. During the interviews, individuals had the opportunity to offer their candid feedback directly to the coach in a manner that protected their anonymity.

A summary report was prepared by the executive coach and shared only with the chief executive. After reviewing and interpreting the report with the help of the executive coach, the chief executive prepared an action plan that he shared with his board members and management team to demonstrate his plans to respond to their suggestions and encourage continuing feedback. While this case applies to a new chief executive encountering resistance, executive coaches can provide all chief executives with opportunities for leadership development, growth, and a safe sounding board that may not be available elsewhere in the organization.

## HOW TO LEARN FROM THE WRONG CHOICE

If the fit between the new chief executive and the organization turns out to be poor enough to warrant a termination, the board should examine the underlying causes for the mismatch before jumping into another search process. The board of an organization whose new chief executive and board agreed to part ways one year after the new chief executive's term began realized that they needed to review lessons learned before trying again. It appointed a senior management professional from within the organization as acting chief executive so the board could explore the following questions before a new chief executive profile was developed:

- What lessons did we learn regarding

    - our selection criteria and process for chief executive selection?

    - our communication with the chief executive?

    - the termination criteria and process?

    - our leadership standards and style preferences?

- What have we learned about

    - our strengths, weaknesses, propensities, and diversity?

    - our group process?

    - our decision-making process?

- What mistakes have we made, and how can we prevent them in the future?

- How can we create greater clarity than we did during the last executive search regarding vision and goals for our next chief executive?

## WARNING SIGNALS OF INADEQUATE SUCCESSION PLANNING

Executive leadership transitions provide golden opportunities for the board to add lasting value. Because this opportunity may be brilliantly disguised as an impossible situation, it is not uncommon for board members to view the executive search process as a job they would prefer not to get stuck with. As a result, they often underplan and underinvest in the parts of the succession planning process that precede the search and selection process.

While succession planning is often deferred until an executive search must be activated, its absence may either foreshadow or reflect the following unfortunate scenarios:

- Crisis resulting from the chief executive's health or personal issues that could or should have been known and acted upon earlier by the board

- Retirement or departure of chief executive delayed because of reluctance of board and/or chief executive to discuss plans and needs in advance

- Dramatic changes resulting in deteriorating staff morale, financial condition, or other measures of organizational performance

- A founder chief executive who is no longer the right leader for the organization.

- High turnover of senior staff members

- Staff and board members who chronically share problems and complaints about the chief executive with others

- A chief executive who has become indispensable and irreplaceable to the organization

- A lack of trust and mutual respect between the board and the chief executive

- A lame duck or incompetent chief executive

- A "monarch" chief executive who demands obedience and delays succession planning

- Inability to make institutional progress as a result of a lack of shared vision and common values between the board and the chief executive

The pundit who once observed that "planning is difficult — especially if it involves the future" — probably had in mind the paradox of succession planning for nonprofit chief executives. After all, it is not the prevailing practice in the nonprofit world for chief executives to groom their successors. Furthermore, chief executives are often reluctant to raise the topic of their career plans for fear of spooking their board members. And board members are often wary of asking their chief executives about their future plans to avoid either alarming them or getting answers they may not like.

The board places a significant bet on the organization's long-term success when it selects the chief executive. The way a board handles this leadership transition will influence the organization's immediate prospects as well its long-term future. Unfortunately, it is seldom possible to predict the precise conditions of each executive transition or to plan every step in advance. It is possible and advisable, however, for the board and the chief executive to talk candidly about the succession planning process on a regular basis and to take the kinds of steps outlined in this book to strengthen the organization's capacity to thrive — regardless of the circumstances surrounding the next executive transition.

One of the most concrete performance indicators for a governing board is the quality of the chief executive it is able to retain as well as to recruit. Succession planning for the chief executive enables the board to have a lasting impact on the success of the organization it governs. When it is done well, it creates the conditions to sustain capable leadership, enhance communications, build healthier relationships, and improve institutional performance through successive leadership transitions. The most effective succession plans are implemented well before there is knowledge of when the incumbent will depart. Imagine how much more could be achieved if boards and chief executives actively and regularly created a legacy for the current and next chief executive to succeed.

## SUCCESSION PLANNING POINTS TO REMEMBER

- Consider establishing a leadership transition team after the new chief executive has been selected.

- Orient the new chief executive in a manner that will help him or her learn the ropes and succeed from the beginning of his or her term.

- Encourage the chief executive to conduct informational interviews with staff members and current and former board members.

- Define the mutual expectations of the board and the chief executive.

- Continue the succession planning cycle once the new chief executive is in place.

- Stay alert to the warning signals of inadequate succession planning.

# APPENDIX 1
## *EMERGENCY LEADERSHIP TRANSITION PLAN*

## A. COMMUNICATIONS PLAN

Who is the first point of contact in the event of a change in the executive director's situation? (Typically, this would be the board chair.)

This person should be prepared to notify all board members and discuss next steps.

Subsequent communication containing the circumstances and recommended plan of action should be sent to all board members for approval and the staff for information.

Once the plan of action has been determined, a message from the board chair should be sent to the organization's key stakeholders detailing the plan for the leadership transition.

## B. FINANCIAL OVERSIGHT

Having multiple signatories on the organization's checking accounts enables business to continue in the chief executive's absence. These signatories might include the chair and the secretary-treasurer (who could also be included on the investment account).

To account for geographical differences, it should be possible to make transactions electronically on all of the accounts.

Contact information for financial advisors should be available for questions related to financial issues.

Contact information for accountants (internal and external) should be available to ensure that timely employee payroll payments are continued.

Other critical information and contact lists should be available to the board chair in the event of an emergency (e.g., contact information for key funders and upcoming deadlines on key activities, such as the deadline for filing the IRS Form 990).

## C. INTERIM MANAGEMENT

Who will the board designate to perform the chief executive's essential duties before the search and selection process has been completed to appoint the permanent chief executive? Should this be determined in advance for short-term periods (e.g., three months) versus longer term periods? Two options for interim management are

1. An acting chief executive appointed by the board to provide leadership during the planning and/or implementation phases of the executive search. This might be a senior manager or a board member.

2. An interim chief executive who helps prepare the organization to work effectively with the next chief executive. This might be a seasoned executive from outside of the organization.

## D. EXECUTIVE SEARCH

While interim management is in place, is the board likely to work with an executive search consultant? If so, what are the best sources of recommendations on qualified search consultants for the board to consider?

What action will the board take to appoint a search committee?

What is the proper delegation of authority between the search committee and the board?

Portions of an emergency leadership transition management plan can be tested when the chief executive takes a vacation, a sabbatical, or some other time away from the organization. This can provide a good opportunity to observe the mettle of emerging leaders within the organization.

# APPENDIX 2
## *CHIEF EXECUTIVE SUCCESSION PLAN GUIDELINES*

Succession planning can strategically position an organization for success before an expected or unforeseen departure of the chief executive. There is no generic template for executive succession planning that will apply to every organization. While the content and timeline of the succession plan should be customized to the circumstances and culture of each organization, the following practices reflect an effective plan.

On an annual basis:

- Create or update an emergency leadership transition plan.

- Conduct a performance review of the chief executive.*

- Assess the chief executive's performance against mutually agreed-upon goals and expectations determined the previous year.

- Implement a process for reviewing the compensation of the chief executive that conforms to the IRS Form 990 and best practice requirements.

- Determine institutional goals and personal goals that the chief executive will be accountable for during the next performance assessment process.

- Clarify expectations between the board and chief executive.

- Ensure that the board and the chief executive have shared goals and a collective vision of how the organization should be evolving over the next three to five years.

- Discuss the chief executive's future plans (regarding term of office).

- Review or update the chief executive job description.

- Determine whether the succession plan should be created, updated, or tweaked.

- Conduct a board self-assessment.*

- Identify the board's strengths and needs.

- Define goals that the board is responsible for implementing.

- Determine how well the board is working with the chief executive.

- Determine actions the board will take to act on the results of the board self-assessment for the purpose of strengthening its structure and practices.

When the chief executive's departure is known:

- Implement emergency leadership transition actions, if necessary.

- Discuss lessons learned by board and staff members who participated in the last chief executive transition process that represent things to repeat or avoid during the next transition.

- Determine whether an interim chief executive or acting chief executive should provide short-term leadership.

- Create a schedule for the executive transition.

- Communicate the executive transition plan with the appropriate constituencies.

- Conduct an organizational assessment to determine leadership needs relevant for next chief executive.

- Convene a search committee to create chief executive profile, recruit candidates, rank applicants, interview candidates, check references, and recommend final candidate(s) to the board.

- Select a new chief executive.

After the new chief executive is selected:

- Create a leadership transition team.

- Implement a communications plan to inform the community of the new appointment.

- Provide a formal orientation for the new chief executive.

- Agree on written goals and expecations for the chief executive.

- Ensure that the expectations and decision-making responsibilities between the board and the chief executive are well delineated.

- Create a timeline for a new succession plan (which defines the role of the board and the chief executive in the process).

* BoardSource offers online board and chief executive assessment tools, as well as detailed analysis and follow-up retreats. www.boardsource.org/BdSA or 800-883-6262 for pricing and more information.

# APPENDIX 3
## *SAMPLE CHIEF EXECUTIVE PROFILE*

## NATIONAL ASSOCIATION OF NONPROFIT CHIEF EXECUTIVE OFFICERS — CHIEF EXECUTIVE PROFILE

The National Association of Nonprofit Chief Executive Officers (NANCEO) is looking for an outstanding individual with strong leadership and management skills to become its next chief executive. NANCEO invites applications from and nominations of candidates with the skills, characteristics, and experience described below. Applications and nominations will be accepted until [date].

## ORGANIZATIONAL BACKGROUND

NANCEO is a national, nonprofit organization based in Chicago whose mission is to advance the effective practices of chief executives for the benefit of the nonprofit organizations they serve. Established 10 years ago by several organizations and nonprofit leaders, NANCEO provides resources, programs, and services to staff leaders, volunteers, corporations, foundations, academic centers, journalists, consultants, and others with an interest in the leadership and management of nonprofit organizations.

NANCEO's programs and services are designed to identify and support effective leadership in the nonprofit sector, promote effective leadership through educational programs and peer networking, and work with partners to promote new models and new approaches to nonprofit leadership. Its key programs and services are

- workshops and training programs for nonprofit leaders to share their experiences and learn from their peers

- leadership and management consultants who work directly with nonprofit organizations to design customized strategies to address an organization's needs

- tools on nonprofit management and governance, including more than 500 booklets, books, videos, CDs, and audiotapes

- an annual conference that brings together more than 1,000 professional and volunteer leaders of nonprofit organizations

## CRITICAL LEADERSHIP ISSUES

The overarching responsibility of the new chief executive is to lead NANCEO to new levels of achievement. NANCEO has enjoyed considerable growth since its creation. It now has more than 100,000 members from the nonprofit community and support from more than 50 foundations, corporations, and individuals. This year, approximately 60 percent of NANCEO's revenue will come from earned income primarily from publications sales, membership dues, and professional development fees. With a budget of $5 million, a staff of 30 and many knowledgeable consultants in the field carry out NANCEO's programs. A 15-member board of directors, comprising individuals who lead and govern nonprofit organizations and bring diverse experience, governs the organization.

The outgoing chief executive of NANCEO, who is departing to pursue new challenges, has been a highly visible and respected leader. The new chief executive will need to build upon the foundation established by the departing chief executive, while exploring new approaches and directions. The new chief executive will be expected to help review NANCEO's core values, its mission, and how it operates in relation to its member, partners, and the general public. He or she will also be expected to aggressively pursue currently successful strategies as well as to identify new opportunities to broaden NANCEO's funding base, increase membership growth, create long-range goals and plans, increase public understanding and visibility of NANCEO's mission and programs, and strengthen its infrastructure.

NANCEO is an extremely vibrant and growing organization that is poised to meet new challenges that NANCEO's chief executive, the nonprofit community, and the profession of nonprofit chief executive officer face. Now more than ever, nonprofit organizations are seeking chief executive officers who can provide leadership and manage the strategic, programmatic, financial, and management operations of their organizations. The rapid pace of change has increased the demand for leaders who can create a climate for learning, innovation, and adaptive change. It has also resulted in increased turnover and shorter terms of service for nonprofit chief executives. NANCEO has the opportunity to grow its programs so that it can serve a larger number of organizations and provide them with a broader array of services to strengthen their capacity to grow, attract, support, and retain effective chief executives.

## KEY RESPONSIBILITIES

The chief executive has the following responsibilities:

1. Serve as NANCEO's most visionary and strategic thinker to anticipate and analyze trends in the field of nonprofit leadership and to work with the board and staff to position the organization to grow and thrive.

2. Support the board and staff to develop a process to create, implement, monitor, and adjust a strategic and tactical plan.

3. Manage a $5 million budget, including developing annual operating budgets that reflect the strategic goals for the organization.

4. Generate revenue by creating new programs, products, and services that support NANCEO's mission and raise funds from current and new foundation, corporate, and individual donors.

5. Provide leadership, guidance, and development to a staff of 30 people.

6. Promote higher public awareness and visibility for the issues confronting nonprofit leaders, including serving as the chief spokesperson and advocate for the organization's mission programs and services.

7. Lead efforts to create new alliances, partnerships, and collaborations with other organizations in the nonprofit, private, and public sectors that will help NANCEO advance its mission.

8. Engage and work in collaboration with the board of directors on matters of governance, mission, vision, and strategy.

9. Expand NANCEO's membership by recruiting new members and retaining existing members.

10. Lead a continuous process of strategic thinking that will enable the board and staff to scan internal and external trends, revisit assumptions and directions, and make meaningful changes in direction as needed.

## DESIRED SKILLS, CHARACTERISTICS, AND COMPETENCIES

The chief executive should have the following professional qualifications and personal characteristics:

1. A keen interest, genuine passion for, and deep personal commitment to NANCEO's mission to advance the effective practice of chief executives for the benefit of the nonprofit organizations they serve.

2. The capacity to facilitate visionary thinking and to articulate a clear, collective vision that will motivate and inspire the staff and board.

3. The ability to develop, motivate, and supervise a committed and talented professional staff and large corps of volunteers who help deliver training programs and other services.

4. The commitment and capacity to engage and support a board that is active and deeply engaged in its role as a fiduciary, steward, and strategic institutional asset.

5. Naturally creative, entrepreneurial, and eager to find innovative ways to launch and sustain new programs and services, reach out to new constituents, and expand NANCEO's vision to new horizons.

6. A strong public presence and the ability to represent NANCEO effectively before a wide range of audiences.

7. Personal qualities of commitment, integrity, and sensitivity to the needs of others.

8. Culturally sensitive and able to work effectively with diverse groups of people.

9. Energetic, self-directed, and well organized to handle multiple tasks, select priorities, and focus on the issues that will contribute most to the growth and success of NANCEO.

10. A good listener and a creative problem solver who is politically savvy, patient, collaborative, and able to reconcile divergent points of view.

11. The ability to honor the past without being inhibited by it.

## IDEAL EXPERIENCE

1. At least 10 years of broad-based senior management experience, including serving as a nonprofit chief executive.

2. A demonstrated track record of building an organization at the national, regional, or local level.

3. A lead role in generating revenue (both earned and contributed income) for an organization as either a volunteer or a professional.

4. Measurable results in hiring, mentoring, developing, leading, and retaining staff and in engaging and supporting a nonprofit governing board.

## COMPENSATION

Salary will be commensurate with experience and qualification. Compensation includes a comprehensive benefits package.

## GUIDELINES FOR CANDIDATES

Nominations and applications should be sent to:

The Search Committee, National Association of Nonprofit Chief Executive Officers, P.O. Box NANCEO, Chicago, Illinois

Candidates should provide a cover letter describing their interest in and qualifications for the position, a résumé, and the names and telephone numbers of five professional references. References will not be contacted until candidates have been notified. For full consideration, materials should be received by [date]. For additional information about NANCEO and this position, please visit our Web site.

# SUGGESTED RESOURCES

Axelrod, Nancy. *Governing for Growth: Using 7 Measures of Success to Strengthen Board Dialogue and Decision Making,* Washington, DC: ASAE & the Center for Association Leadership, 2009.

Bell, Jeanne, Richard Moyers, and Timothy Wolfred. *Daring to Lead 2006: A National Study of Nonprofit Executive Leadership.* CompassPoint and Eugene and Agnes E. Meyer Foundation, 2006, www.compasspoint.org/assets/194_daringtolead06final.pdf

BoardSource. *Nonprofit Governance Index 2007.* Washington, DC: BoardSource, 2007.

BoardSource. *The Source: Twelve Principles of Governance That Power Exceptional Boards.* Washington, DC: BoardSource, 2005.

Collingwood, Harris (editor). "Breakthrough Leadership." *Harvard Business Review,* Special Issue, December 2001.

Drucker, Peter F. *The Drucker Foundation Self-Assessment Tool for Nonprofit Organizations.* San Francisco: Jossey-Bass, Inc., 1993.

Goleman, Daniel. *Emotional Intelligence: Why It Can Matter More than IQ.* New York: Bantam, 1995.

Herman, Robert D., and Richard D. Heimovics. *Executive Leadership in Nonprofit Organizations.* San Francisco: Jossey-Bass, Inc., 1991.

Hesselbein, Frances, Marshall Goldsmith, and Richard Beckhard. *The Leader of the Future.* San Francisco: Jossey-Bass, Inc., 1996.

Ingram, Richard T. *Ten Basic Responsibilities of Nonprofit Boards, Second Edition.* Washington, DC: BoardSource, 2009.

McLaughlin, Tom and Addie Nelson Backlund. *Moving Beyond Founder's Syndrome to Nonprofit Success.* Washington, D.C. BoardSource, 2008.

Moyers, Richard L. *The Nonprofit Chief Executive's Ten Basic Responsibilities.* Washington, D.C.: BoardSource, 2006.

Peters, Jeanne, and Timothy Wolfred. *Daring To Lead: Nonprofit Executive Directors and Their Work Experience.* San Francisco: CompassPoint Nonprofit Services, 2001.

Pierson, Jane, and Joshua Mintz. *Assessment of the Chief Executive: A Tool for Nonprofit Boards.* Washington, DC: BoardSource, 2005.

Rosen, Robert H. *Leading People.* New York: Penguin Books, 1997.

Simon, Judith Sharken. *The Five Life Stages of Nonprofit Organizations: Where You Are, Where You're Going, and What to Expect When You Get There.* Saint Paul, MN: The Amherst H. Wilder Foundation, 2001.

Tebbe, Don. *Chief Executive Transitions: How to Hire and Support a Nonprofit CEO.* Washington, DC: BoardSource, 2009.

The Bridgespan Group. *Finding Leaders for America's Nonprofits.* The Bridgespan Group, 2009, www.bridgespan.org/finding-leaders-for-americas-nonprofits.aspx

Twombly, Eric C. and Marie G. Gantz. *Executive Compensation in the Nonprofit Sector: New Findings and Policy Implications.* Washington, DC: The Urban Institute, 2001.

Vogel, Brian, and Charles W. Quatt, Ph.D. *Nonprofit Executive Compensation: Planning, Performance, and Pay, Second Edition.* Washington, DC: BoardSource, 2010.

Wertheimer, Mindy R. *The Board Chair Handbook.* Washington, DC: BoardSource, 2008.

Williams, Sherill K. and Kathleen A. McGinnis. *Getting the Best From Your Board: An Executive's Guide to a Successful Partnership.* Washington, DC: BoardSource, 2007.

# ABOUT THE AUTHOR

Nancy R. Axelrod is a governance consultant who provides services to nonprofit organizations in board education, development, self-assessment, and leadership transitions. She frequently serves as a speaker at leadership forums dedicated to governance and accountability. Axelrod has served as a governing and advisory board member and board development consultant to numerous associations, foundations, charitable organizations, higher education institutions, and other nonprofit organizations. She is a member of the faculty of the Institute for Board Chairs and Presidents of Independent Colleges and Universities, sponsored by the Association of Governing Boards of Universities and Colleges, and ASAE & the Center for Association Leadership's Exceptional Boards program.

Axelrod is the founding president of the National Center for Nonprofit Boards (now known as BoardSource), where she served as its first chief executive officer from 1987 to 1996. She is the author of *Culture of Inquiry: Healthy Debate in the Boardroom; Governing for Growth: Using 7 Measures of Success to Strengthen Board Dialogue and Decision Making;* and *Advisory Councils.* She is a contributing author to *The Jossey-Bass Handbook of Nonprofit Leadership and Management* and has written numerous articles and op-ed pieces. Axelrod currently serves as a member of the advisory board of the Initiative on Social Enterprise at the Harvard Business School and the review panel of the NACD Director of the Year Award. She is a former chairman of the board of trustees of the Association Leadership Foundation of the Greater Washington Society of Association Executives. She can be reached at www.nancyaxelrod.com.